A VIEW THROUGH THE FOG

BOB MCGEE

Copyright 2023 by MSI Press LLC

All rights reserved. No part of this book may be reproduced or utilized in any form or by any means, electronic or mechanical, including photocopying and recording, or by any information storage and retrieval system without permission in writing from the publisher.

For information, contact

MSI Press, LLC

1760-F Airline Hwy #203

Hollister, CA 95023

Copyeditor: Betty Lou Leaver

Cover design & layout: Opeyemi Ikuborije

Front cover photo: Alexander Steamaze

Photo credits:

   Bob McGee: chapters 1, 2, 3, 4, 5, 6, 7, 8, 10, 11, 12, 13, 17, 18

   Shutterstock: chapters 9 (Dan Lewis), 4 (Steve Buckley), 15 (Aaron Finn), 16 (Photo_Time)

Library of Congress Control Number: 2023938032

ISBN: 9781957354279

CONTENTS

Dedication i

Acknowledgement iii

Introduction v

First Days 1

A Long Way Down 9

The Shacks 13

Condos 23

Scooters 31

Women Jump, Too 41

The Boneyard 45

South Tower Legs 53

One Size Fits All 59

Jumpers Throughout The Years 63

Tower Shower 69

South Tower Pier 75

Unpredictable Behaviors 83

Strut Four 89

Strut Four Revisited 97

Prevention Protocol. 103

The Nav Project 113

Last Goodbye 121

Appendix A: Glossary/Bridge Terms 129

Appendix B: Bridge Statistics 131

Dedication

This book is lovingly dedicated to my wife, who has tolerated my quirks far longer than any person should ever have to. Eternal thanks, Debbie.

Acknowledgement

Many thanks to Betty Lou Leaver, Opeyemi Ikuborije, and the rest of the staff at MSI Press. I have grown as a writer due to Betty's uncompromising standards. She challenges me at every turn and drove me to earn this book. Had it not been for Betty, *A View through the Fog* would not exist.

I also want to thank my extraordinary line editor, Clare Jordan, for her remarkable patience, top-notch editing skills, and for always being there to guide me through the editing process.

Next, this book would not be what it is without the marvelous editing assistance from three great professionals; Olivia Eisinger, Michaela Fair, and Kristen Hamilton.

Special thanks to Lorri Ungaretti, Mimi Towle, and Anca-Maria Chirita who trusted my writing enough to find a place for my stories among the pages of their wonderful publications.

Last but not least, I want to thank my parents for teaching me I can be whatever I want to be, as long as I'm willing to put in the work and effort to get there.

And of course, my wife, who has been there for me since we began, a long time ago. Love you Deb.

Introduction

Heading southbound through the Robin Williams Tunnel, formerly the Waldo Tunnel, on the way to the Golden Gate Bridge humbles the soul nearly any morning as the strikingly beautiful San Francisco skyline greets workers and visitors alike. A privileged encounter with sun and sea! On the left, the radiating orb rising over the East Bay Hills quietly lays its rays upon Alcatraz Island. On the right, the picturesque Marin Headlands quietly yield to the endless expanse of the Pacific Ocean. Scattered clouds in the sky above cast their silhouettes upon the towers of the Bridge.

On a foggy day, the Bridge develops its own distinct environment: a white mist creeps along the Bridge, slowly wrapping its arms around everyone and everything that moves, leading all into a shifting fog bank. This thick white wall, accompanied by the eerie call of the Bridge foghorns, gives the illusion that this mass of concrete and steel is perhaps a living entity.

Clouds follow along her sidewalk from high in the sky, creating an interplay of light and shadow upon the Bridge's towers. The gentle morning mist blankets everything in fog, teasing the senses with a faint chill that almost isn't there. Energy flows through the muted steel, and a hush fills the emptiness, like a voice waiting to speak.

Hours later she gets attention in other ways, channeling gusts of wind that tear through the body one after the other, relentlessly, a reminder that great power lies behind her great beauty—a clinging wind unwilling to let go.

She has given me views of San Francisco Bay that are absolutely breathtaking. She has shared evenings with me on her South Tower, showing me dazzling sights of the city or the rising moon breaking through the clouds at midnight over the ocean. These experiences always thrilled me with a delight that I never tired of and will never forget. I used to think about how lucky I was that Bridge Management did not know they were actually paying me to do a job I would no doubt have done for free.

Still one of the most recognized structures in the world, the Golden Gate Bridge is visited by more than nine million tourists and admirers every year. With views very familiar, yet unique to every facet of the Bridge's environment, the Bridge ages, yet her popularity never wanes.

I dreamed of being a painter on the Golden Gate Bridge for many reasons. The Bridge is a tremendous achievement in both design and construction. What an honor to be responsible for keeping this architectural treasure safe in my hands! Constant maintenance from a permanent paint crew is required to dress the Bridge with a coat of International Orange, protecting her from the natural erosions of wind and fog, along with the constant exposure of her steel to the salty sea air. It is the most glorious job for any painter even though the job amounts to no more than licking her wounds, and I was more than willing to risk life and limb to do my part to keep her standing forever.

When I was a young boy in the 1970's, my dad and grandpa took me fishing off the shores at the North End under the Bridge. For the first time, I heard the deafening whistles from the sandblasters that open-blasted the steel on the Bridge above. I witnessed sand shooting everywhere, and I watched the spent sand flowing down the rocky cliffs into huge piles on the path near where we were fishing. The distinct flinty smell of sand dust filled the air as it wafted out over the bay. The noise, the sand, the smell, the fog... what an impression it all made on me! I knew then, even at that young age, that this was where I wanted to work when I was older.

In those days, open blasting was a common practice. Environmental restrictions on sandblasting did not exist; containing the toxic spent sand and paint chips was not a requirement. All that kept me from jumping into those piles of sand that had streamed down the cliffs were my dad and grandpa's continued warnings that the sand was contaminated and unsafe. They would certainly know as they were both retired painters who had spent their careers painting steel in shipyards and oil refineries.

They had no desire for me to follow in their footsteps. Steel painting is not an easy living, but when all other avenues in my life had been exhausted, I became a painter. It was in my blood and seemed to be my destined path. I toiled for years painting in oil refineries and on other bridges around the San Francisco Bay until finally, in 2003, I landed my dream job as a painter on the Golden Gate Bridge.

The popular image of what we did for a living was largely a myth, one that we had no shame indulging. While I worked at the Bridge, there were televised episodes about us on *National Geographic, Modern Marvels,* and *California's Gold*. Even *Good Morning America* filmed a live segment that included some of our painters on the top of the North Tower.

This type of coverage, along with what the public could witness themselves, sustained the image that our job differed greatly from most jobs. Painters were filmed casually straddling the main cable 700 feet above the water or riding on a swing stage along the sides of the towers in perilous weather conditions. Even our proximity to suicide jumpers added to the mystique of our job. We were fearless, swashbuckling protectors of the steel.

I always enjoyed the privilege of interacting with so many tourists and visitors throughout the years. I am asked a variety of questions about my years at the Bridge, but often the same ones come up repetitively, making the answers also repetitious: "Yes, that is Alcatraz Prison; the color of the bridge is International Orange; an elevator in each tower goes to the top; no, we do not paint the bridge from one end to the other, then start again..." These kinds of conversations became part of our daily routine as Bridge painters.

Another not-so-trivial subject often inquired about by visitors to the Bridge and a question still asked today when people find out what I did for a living, is "What do you know about suicide jumpers?"

No doubt, suicide jumpers come to mind when one thinks of the Golden Gate Bridge. Questions concerning this subject may be asked out of harmless morbid curiosity. Or, perhaps, misconception and urban myths fuel them, leading people to believe that earthquakes and suicide jumps happen there every day, which, of course, is not true.

Thousands of tourists from all over the planet flock to the Golden Gate Bridge each day, but it is no secret that the Bridge's intrigue, mystique, and popularity also attract another element: those looking to end their lives in a romanticized manner by jumping from this famous landmark. I do not intend to analyze the psychological reasons why a person leaps from the Bridge because I know little about the subject. If the Bridge knows why people jump, she is unable to tell her secrets, so I will do my best to share with you all I have witnessed regarding jumpers. Along the way, I will try to answer some questions I've been asked about suicide jumps at the Golden Gate Bridge.

The Bridge is a national monument, so state and federal agencies funded most of our maintenance painting. This job had it all: the best training, a powerful union, great pay, and super benefits. The job appeared to be rock solid, but internally, the Paint Department began crumbling from the decay of years past, caused by complacency, arrogance, neglect, and greed.

I painted at the Golden Gate Bridge for 12 years, a small window of time in the storied history of the painters on the Bridge, but it was an important time because it marked the breakdown of our power structure, the end of an era. Luxuries and perks that had ruled the Paint Department for many years were being systematically extinguished by Bridge Management.

As employees, we were granted a surprising amount of freedom to operate. A private culture facilitated by our own grandiosity had long reigned within this world of seasoned veterans. The egotism that sprang from our outmoded habits gave rise to an arrogance that blinded us to the realities and truths of the entitled environment we had created.

Survival depends upon adaptability; a reluctance to change some of the old ways and outdated traditions led to the Department's decline. Self-awareness had slipped away. By the time we finally realized that our flamboyant customs were leading to our demise, it was too late.

I believe what happened behind the scenes at the Bridge was infinitely more interesting than the exaggerated myth that dominates mainstream thought. We were a diverse ensemble of individuals and crews, all bound by a sense of loyalty both to each other and to the job. The real Paint Department was a place where workers lost their tempers, cracked jokes, and even fought, where each crew jealously guarded its turf, and where slipups and misunderstandings were common. I knew these workers professionally and personally, and this was a place where I fit right in.

I will not fill this book with facts and statistics that can easily be found in many other publications about the Bridge. In recreating my experiences, I don't want the narrative to suffocate under a mass of technical detail and conjecture. However, for those readers who need to quench a thirst for Bridge facts and figures, I have added an appendix at the end of this book, which I hope you enjoy.

I have the advantage of being an amateur storyteller. My intention is to present a unique firsthand look at how we operated as high steel painters on the Golden Gate Bridge. I have made every effort to portray the events exactly as they occurred and to record, as accurately as possible, the actions of the painters who lived them. The more intimately we observe the essence of human habits, emotions, and responses, the better understanding we have of our subject. Writers do not always possess deeply personal insights about the world they are trying to describe. This was obviously not the case with me, and my aim here is to describe this world I know so well in a way that will make readers feel they are on the main cable with me.

CHAPTER 1

FIRST DAYS

I'm in heaven, walking the cable on my second day.

A VIEW THROUGH THE FOG

The late afternoon Bay Area breeze knows no season. My once white coveralls, now stained with red-oxide primer, helped take the bite away from the piercing April air, allowing me to become lost in the remarkable view of the Carquinez Straits as I looked out from the catwalk below the Benicia Bridge.

The sound of soft-soled work boots approaching me on the catwalk interrupted my reflective moment of solitude. Taking up the same pose as me, arms crossed, leaning across the top guard-rail of the catwalk, my paint foreman Don shared the view for a moment before whispering, "The Gate is hiring painters."

My concentration broke, and I immediately turned my gaze on Don. Still facing out toward the straits, he said, "There's three openings, but you've only got two days to get the paperwork in." Then, he added, "Just something to think about."

The timing of this opportunity couldn't have been better. I love working on bridges. For years, I had painted bridges from one end of California to the other, but after two years on the Benicia Bridge, the routine had become tedious. A great job, but just a job, nonetheless. The thrill had dissipated. Perhaps it was time for a move. I'm guessing Don sensed this feeling in me.

He took one last look at the view, breathed deeply, and began the half-mile walk down the catwalk toward the abutment when suddenly he turned and held a finger up as if he'd remembered one last point, "Oh, and probably best to keep this to yourself. Most of your competition will probably come from the painters on this bridge—and don't misunderstand the situation: it will be a competition."

Nodding thoughtfully, I thanked Don again, and went back to my casual lean on the rail, but now there was much more on my mind than just the view. I considered the foundations of my love for bridge painting: the work, the view, the challenge, and, of course, the pay. The Golden Gate Bridge excelled in all these aspects, and wasn't working on this marvelous structure the reason I'd become a bridge painter in the first place? As I made my way down the catwalk that afternoon, I was all smiles with dreams of grandeur. I knew that the Golden Gate Bridge provided one thing above all—glory!

Openings within the Golden Gate Bridge Paint Department only occur about once every decade. These openings are often in such high demand that their existence is guarded with secrecy—perhaps by Bridge Management who have favorites they hope to fill the positions or maybe by painters from the outside who do not want competition from fellow workers. I was lucky to get the heads up, and I applied just in time.

Despite the deliberate covertness, there were still hundreds of applicants for the three spots. The job prerequisites were tough, and after six weeks of screening, 16 applicants were chosen for the next phase of the hiring process: a full day of hands-on testing, followed by an oral interview the next day. This would result in six finalists, three of whom would be offered a painter position at the Golden Gate Bridge.

The first day of testing involved displaying our technical knowledge and efficiency at three separate stations: a sandblast station, a spray paint booth, and a knot-tying station.

This was not a problem for me as I was well experienced in these tasks. The next day was where my worries lay. I faced a one-hour oral interview conducted by two bridge officials, the paint superintendent, and a union mediator acting as a representative for fair hiring practices.

After this stressful process concluded, I had received the second-highest score, which was good enough for one of the positions. All that remained was a background check, an intense physical, a drug-screening test, and five months of impatiently waiting for the number two spot to open. It was an anxious but wonderful five months.

With my new job secured, it was time to give notice at the Benicia Bridge. I approached the Bridge's paint supervisor, who, according to what I had heard, didn't think the job opening at the Golden Gate would be a good fit for me. "A few years before, I spent six months on loan as a steel inspector for the Golden Gate Bridge," he told me and began recounting what he had seen while working there.

Walking past the painters' break room every morning, he said, he'd often smell bacon being fried during work hours. "Painters would sometimes wait days for the weather to change and do nothing but spend that time in their painters' shacks, polishing rivets and whittling duck decoys!"

If the reasons he gave were meant to make me doubt my decision to work at the Golden Gate, he could not have been more wrong. I laughed and let him know that I absolutely loved bacon. "Plus," I pointed out, "why would you assume I wouldn't enjoy polishing rivets and whittling duck decoys?" I thanked him rather sarcastically for watching out for me, but despite his warnings, I knew I was about to start the greatest job of my life.

After a long five months, I was at last a Golden Gate Bridge painter. The Paint Department included a paint superintendent, five crew foremen, twenty-six bridge painters, five paint laborers, and two apprentice painters. It was a very experienced group. At 39 years old, I was the youngest painter in the Department.

On the first day, I met Rocky, the Paint Superintendent. The Paint Department definitely belonged to him. A wiseass with a somewhat warped sense of humor, he was generally easygoing and a good guy. A longtime painter on the Bridge himself, he approved and enforced Paint Department traditions. He did not want any troubles within the Department to hit his desk. Basically, if you didn't give him extra paperwork and certainly didn't embarrass him in the eyes of management or other departments, then you would be fine.

The Paint Superintendent before Rocky had held the position for many years and was a well-liked leader until his reign came to a horrible end. He was found dead at the Bridge early one morning. He had hanged himself in one of the storage bunkers.

Rocky went over basic protocol for my first day: showing me the sign-in/sign-out sheet, which was to be signed in the morning when we arrived and each afternoon before we left. This was a means of monitoring a painter's whereabouts. "Painters had become too carefree, just sneaking off at any time during the day to go home," he said, pointing at the sheet. "This is an official way of curbing painter attendance problems."

I tried to search out his eyes with mine, but no contact came. His expression gave every indication that he was serious about painters leaving the job. He continued to speak, but for a few long moments, the words that followed were just babble to my ears as I envisioned painters moving stealthily through the parking lot, wearing high-collared trench coats and ball caps pulled down low, creeping to their cars and speeding off the bridge in all directions. Shaking myself loose from these thoughts, I reentered the conversation and dutifully nodded my assent. I felt a strong urge to discuss this further with him, but not now.

Rocky just needed an official record showing that painters were where they were supposed to be, one of the many forms of CYA (Cover Your Ass) that existed on the Bridge. This was still not enough to keep painters from finding ways to totally screw up even the simplest of job regulations.

When I started at the Bridge, the sign-out sheet would be posted at 3:20 pm even though our official quitting time was 3:30 pm, granting us ten minutes to get to our cars. This was a privilege that ended one afternoon soon after I'd arrived. One of our more impulsive painters signed out at 3:20 pm, jumped into his car, sped off, and made it all the way to Lombard Street in San Francisco before he accidentally struck and killed a pedestrian. Official time of death? 3:29 pm.

The death occurred while the painter was still officially on the clock. The Paint Department took a lot of heat for this, and as a result, sign-out time was now set forward to 3:25 pm. The irony of this was that there was more uproar in the Department about the loss of those five minutes of grace time than the loss of a person's life.

Later that first day, Rocky took me on a tour of our facilities at the toll plaza. We descended into the underground military bunkers, which stored much of our paint and equipment. These areas were old and had served troops during World War II, with some rooms even dating as far back as the Civil War. As I entered the maze of bunkers for the first time, stale, moldy air immediately greeted my lungs, and coupled with the eye-watering pungency of ammonia, caused an involuntary gasp. As I dried my eyes and regained my composure, though, I realized that the dank atmosphere of the bunkers only added to their eerie appeal.

Rocky brought me to the infamous beam from which his predecessor had hanged himself. My skin crawled as I circled beneath the beam. Examining it with curious wonder, I imagined what might be going on in Rocky's mind. My gaze switched to Rocky, whose face betrayed no emotion. I wanted to ask questions about the former superintendent's suicide: Did he commit suicide because of his job? Should this be a warning of what I might be in for? But I knew this was not the time. Rocky just stared at the beam for a long moment before we moved on. Later, I would find out there wasn't much known about the suicide other than it being an apparently spontaneous act committed by a seemingly stable family man. I avoided this area of the bunker for the rest of my years at the Bridge.

Next stop was "Stores." This was a mini warehouse set up as a means of supplying Bridge employees with anything they needed for the job. The facility resembled a small hardware store and offered unlimited tools, safety clothing, paint supplies, office supplies, and sundries. If it could be used at the Bridge, you could probably find it at Stores. In fact, I once lost a bet when a painter actually walked out of there with a machete and a pitchfork!

All we had to do was give the shopkeeper our Bridge ID and then shop away. Obviously, acquiring store items for personal use was not allowed, but excessive abuse of Stores was something of a norm at the Bridge. Some painters would show up to work with empty backpacks and leave with them jammed full every day. One afternoon, I saw a painter heading to his car. He was wearing a thick coat but still looked as if he had gained a lot of weight since I'd seen him earlier in the day. When he spotted me, he raised a finger to his lips, then opened his coat to reveal a huge clear bag full of plastic forks and spoons. He zipped the coat back up, proudly smiled, and kept walking. I shook my head, incredulous. This guy made a lot of money working at the Bridge, yet he would risk getting caught and losing his job for fifteen dollars' worth of plastic utensils.

After a tour of the yard, Rocky took me onto the Bridge in his paint scooter. He told me that the East Sidewalk, which faces the bay, was open to tourists and bicyclists. The West Sidewalk, facing the ocean, was for Bridge workers only. We took to the East Sidewalk first. "Dealing with tourists is an important part of our job," he explained. He insisted that I be courteous, take time to answer their questions, and try to make their visit to the Bridge as enjoyable as possible.

During my years at the Bridge, I never had a problem with this part of the job and enjoyed interacting with tourists. At times, I felt no different than one who had been hired to wear a Mickey Mouse costume and roam Disneyland might feel posing for selfies, pointing the way to the restrooms, and letting kids stomp your feet. Tourist interaction was a simple means of expressing my love for the Bridge. This made my job more than "just a job" and enabled me to become a part of the tourists' Bridge experience.

Now, it was time to meet my new crew. The members of the South Tower Crew were known affectionately as Tiller, Stew, Robin, Smokey, Kevin, Junior, and Mike. Each painter I met was very welcoming and treated me like family, making it feel more like a fraternity than a workplace. Some I had met or worked with before, and some were legendary painters whose names I had heard many times over the years. These were men I would be around each and every workday for years. Mike was assigned as my work partner on day one and remained my partner until I retired 12 years later.

The first day was filled with advice from different painters I met: "Remember to forget everything you ever knew about painting," "Just don't tell your wife what goes on here," and my favorite, "Sit back and relax, you now work for the Golden Goose." What a great first day!

When I clocked out that day, I realized I could not wait to come back in the morning. I saw much on my first day I could not yet comprehend and had more questions than answers, but I decided to just go forward with an open mind and immerse myself in my new job.

My second day working at the Bridge was warm and sunlit. A man once told me there were only 13 days a year when the weather is perfect in San Francisco—sunny, clear, and virtually no wind. This was one of those 13 days.

First thing that morning, my new boss Rocky had me grab my harness and lanyards. He told me to go see one of the operating engineers, who instructed me to put my body harness on, telling me I would need both my lanyards for where we were heading. "Are you ready?" he asked.

"Absolutely," I replied, trying not to show the curiosity or the anxiety I felt.

He laughed. "You have no clue what we are going to do, huh?"

"Nope. I decided to open my mind to anything new here, and I'm just gonna enjoy the experience!"

"Okay, I like that," he said. "Well, then, I won't spoil the surprise for you, but you're going to love what's coming up."

I smiled, and we climbed in his Bridge scooter and headed out to the West Sidewalk to mid-span, where the main cables reached their lowest point. He untied a 12-foot extension ladder from the outer rail, leaning it against the lowest point of the main cable and turned to me. "Are you afraid of heights?"

"Afraid of heights? No," I answered, "afraid of falling, yes. I'm scared to death, so I respect every second I work up high."

"Good," he nodded.

I had worked heights my whole painting career and had been to the top of every other bridge in the area, but I knew this would be different. Just how different I had yet to find out. I climbed up onto the main cable, hooked in both lanyards, and we began ascending from mid-span to the North Tower. Footing on the cable was surprisingly more secure than I'd expected, but the upward angle of the cable was much steeper than it had seemed.

Not even halfway into the 500-foot climb, exhaustion began setting in. Foolishly underestimating the angle of the cable, I had used all my energy early in the climb, trying to keep up with the operating engineer. My upper body tensed from the tight grip I maintained on the safety cables, which acted as a handrail. A slight burning sensation spread through my thighs, and my multi-layered clothing was doing me no favors as I became overheated and began to sweat.

I felt as though I needed a brief rest. As I raised my head and glanced up at the engineer, though, I realized there would be no stopping on this climb. Not a glimmer of sweat on his face, only determination in his eyes. As I watched him gracefully unclipping and reattaching his lanyard hooks at the vertical post situated at every 30 feet of the handrail, it was obvious he had made this climb at least 100 times.

He had not looked back at me in the last ten minutes, and I doubted he even remembered I was behind him. Was his speed actually picking up as he neared the top? I stopped, smiled, shook my head, and took a deep breath before pressing onward. Had it not been for my excitement and adrenaline, the trek up the cable probably would have beaten me.

The operating engineer reached the top of the North Tower first, and just before I caught up to him, he took out his camera and snapped a photo of me. I have examined the photo often, They say a picture tells a thousand words. Well, this photo of me is still a word short because there is no way a mere photo could ever capture the pure exhilaration and elation I felt at that moment.

I climbed onto the tower top, went to its center, and began turning slowly in a circle to catch every angle of the unobstructed dream view, 700 feet above it all. The City, the Bay, the Headlands, the ocean—it was all here in front of my eyes. The sweet and overpowering beauty of it excited a sensation of joy in me, one where reality and dream coexist, and breathing becomes something that takes effort to do. I leaned my hands on my knees, catching my breath, shaking my head, and laughing to myself.

"Amazing," I said, glancing up at him while still bent over. "A few more minutes, if it's okay with you?"

He nodded, and a few minutes turned into half an hour. I just could not get enough of the experience, but he understood because he loved the Bridge as I did.

Eventually, the operating engineer put a hand on my shoulder, and in a soft voice he told me it was time to head back down. After drawing a huge breath of the cool, salty air, I took one last scan of the glorious view before submitting with a humble nod.

Descending the cable was quite another experience. "Whoa," I breathed, careful not to slip. The incline was even more evident heading down and at some points seemed like a straight drop. In order to restrict myself from too fast a pace, I had to tightly grip the safety cables the entire way.

When I reached the bottom of the cable at mid-span, I looked down at my gloved hands. Both had been so severely chafed from the descent that the gloves now had palm-sized holes in them.

I was buzzing all that day from my cable climb, an experience very few are ever privileged to have and one extremely hard to express in words. I am smiling even right now as I write this.

By the end of my second day at the Bridge, I no longer had questions in need of answering. I was a changed man after my main cable walk to the North Tower. The Bridge had successfully used her beauty and charm to take possession of my soul, and her subtle spirit had bent me to her will. I belonged to her now.

CHAPTER 2

A LONG WAY DOWN

a long way down

A VIEW THROUGH THE FOG

If you've worked on the Golden Gate Bridge long enough, you have probably seen at least one person go over the outer rail, heard a splash from someone hitting the water, or glimpsed the body of an unfortunate jumper floating in the bay. To witness an entire jump, though, is a rare occurrence. Something like being in the wrong place at the wrong time.

It was May 2004, a sunny morning on the Bridge. Robin and I had been tasked with painting below the Bridge atop the west end of the South Tower Pier. The piers are the massive concrete bases that support the legs of both the North and South Towers. The piers extend perpendicularly away from the Bridge, outward across the water. The tops of the piers sit approximately 44 feet above sea level. Surrounding the South Tower Pier is an oval shaped concrete fender that acts as both a breakwater and a barrier to keep ships from colliding with the tower. Between the pier and this outer fender is a moat filled with seawater that flows freely in and out.

Working on that pier always gave me a unique perspective of the Bridge, as if I were on my own little concrete island in the middle of the bay, blessed with incredible views of San Francisco, Alcatraz, the East Bay, Fort Point, and Marin County that most never see. I enjoyed these sights from the pier for years.

On this particular morning, the unforgettable sight came from above. A call came over our portable Bridge radio that a distressed man was pacing the East Sidewalk between the South Tower and mid-span. Talking with Bridge Authorities for two hours on his cell phone, he was contemplating a jump off the Bridge and threatening to do it if anyone approached him. Our position on the pier allowed us a clear view of the East Sidewalk's outer rail. The rail stood about 200 feet above us and about 240 feet above the water. But unable to see the man on the sidewalk, Robin and I returned to our project on the pier, hoping for a resolution to the negotiation standoff above.

Suddenly, Robin grabbed my arm, diverting my attention to a man with long hair sitting on the outer rail about a hundred yards north of the South Tower, toward mid-span. From my vantage point, he appeared calm, perched on the rail with his back to us, casually talking on his cell phone. After watching him for several minutes, I doubted his intention to jump since he'd had plenty of time to contemplate his inevitable fate if he did.

I glanced away for just a moment, then heard Robin yell, "Oh s___, he's jumping!" I immediately looked up to see the man already falling feet first with his back to us and his arms stretched out above his head. Even though he traveled downward extremely fast, the four seconds it took him to reach the water seemed so much longer. I cannot imagine how long those four seconds must have felt to him..

One... man falling.
The man did not scream as he plummeted to the water, but I remember hearing his clothes flapping loudly.

Two... man still falling.
His shirt and undershirt peeled away from his body. They wrapped around his head, ready to fly off his wrists as he neared the water.

Three... man still falling

Four... man hits water.
His impact with the water caused an enormous splash, followed by the most defining moment of the jump—the sound.

During the first few months that I worked at the Bridge, I would look down from the sidewalk at that 240-foot drop and wonder why more people did not survive the jump. It didn't look like a fatal distance from above, especially with calm waters on a pleasant day. Watching this man collide with the water forever ended all such notions for me.

The splash and the sound that followed shocked me, which I can only liken to a shotgun blast. My entire body cringed away from this sick sound, an unforgettable sound, one that told me this man's body had been broken in so many ways. Undoubtedly, the man did not survive. I closed my eyes, knowing, at that exact second, that I had witnessed a death.

From my elevated position atop the pier, I could see the victim less than a hundred yards away, drifting along in a swift current. He remained submerged 3-4 feet below the water's surface, surrounded by a ring of blood. A sobering sight.

Shortly thereafter, a smoking kettle that signifies the location of a jump came crashing down into the water near the body. Alerted to the possibility of a jump, the US Coast Guard wasted no time in getting to the scene. Unfortunately, no rescue or resuscitation would be needed upon their arrival, only the retrieval of a broken body.

A jumble of emotions overwhelmed me: at once I felt astonished, humbled, and sad. My misconception that someone could survive a jump from the sidewalk ended in an instant. Bridge workers later impressed upon me the rarity of witnessing an entire jump as I had, but I did not feel privileged. Although I had never met the man who was later identified as Gene Sprague, I feel sorrow even today for having witnessed his passing.

CHAPTER 3

THE SHACKS

*Our sandblast work station on the west sidewalk at midspan.
The paint shacks were scattered along this sidewalk,
which was off limits to tourists.*

A VIEW THROUGH THE FOG

Weather conditions often made it impossible to work on the Bridge, forcing painters to wait out the wind, rain, or fog in compact spaces known as the shacks. Time spent in these unregulated spaces quickly introduced one of the most unusual aspects of my job as a painter on the Golden Gate. Already having been introduced to a few amazing job perks, I felt there must be a catch attached to this one. If a thing appears too good to be true, it usually is.

On my second day at the Bridge, my crew foreman assigned me a shack. He didn't bother to conceal a smile when he told me who my permanent shack mate would be, and the rest of the crew snickered. I'd already met this new shack partner of mine and knew why everyone thought it was so funny, but you'll get to know about Smokey soon enough. At that moment, I was still trying to wrap my mind around what the heck a shack was for.

Nobody on the crew had bothered to explain these shacks to me. As the crew jumped into their scooters and headed to the shacks, I just rode along. Kevin sat beside me. He had started about six months earlier and was the applicant who placed number one in our group of three new hires. I had known Kevin for about 15 years, and he had always seemed trustworthy. Once we'd arrived, he sensed my confusion, took me aside, and explained the official purpose of the shacks was to give painters a place to shelter during adverse weather conditions. I nodded, telling him I understood what their function was, then carefully added that I couldn't help but notice this morning's weather was just fine. He laughed at the obvious bemusement on my face and told me to relax and clear my head of all I ever knew about painting. Just go with this one and enjoy it for what it was. It was good advice, and this would not be the last time I would hear it from other painters over the next couple of months. It eventually became my favorite way of advising other new painters.

High wind speeds were deemed dangerous, but there was no other official description of unsuitable weather conditions barring us from work on the Bridge. The existing guidelines were often scrutinized and subject to interpretation. Usually, anything over 20 mph winds would be unsafe. Fog forms excessive moisture in the air, keeping the steel surface wet and unsuited for paint, as well as making it hazardous to walk. Rain creates an obviously harsh work environment.

Anyone who knows the Bridge understands the weather conditions on the bay are rarely ideal and often unstable. This created opportunity for painters not only regularly to use the shacks for shelter from adverse weather but also habitually to take advantage of loose guidelines, often claiming the weather to be too inclement to work. Though I was lucky enough to belong to a paint crew that would brave some questionable weather-related circumstances for a job needing to be done, more often than not, we spent our days in the shacks along with the other painters.

Some projects required ironworkers to go out before us and replace lacings, bolts, wind braces, and so on. They would rig most of the swing stages, baskets, floats, and platforms we worked from, sometimes leading us to alternate painting jobs inside the towers, shielded from bad Bridge weather. Yet, when such jobs were not needed, back to shacks we would go, to wait.

In theory, the shacks served as a sanctuary for painters as they waited for weather to break, fog to lift, repairs to be made, or rigging to be set, always prepared to return to work on short notice. That much I understood.

The West Sidewalk was used exclusively by Bridge personnel, so there were no tourists allowed. There were 15 paint shacks on the West Sidewalk, three at each end of the span, and nine between the two towers, each like a blemish on a beautiful face. All were painted International Orange to match the color of the Bridge but nonetheless represented a failed attempt at camouflage. They obstructed a fine view from the Bridge to the ocean and were an eyesore on a bridge otherwise known for her aesthetic beauty.

Each crew was assigned three shacks situated in groups along the sidewalk. Abutting the back rail, they gave just enough room for our paint scooters to pass by on the sidewalk. Each shack, about 8' × 4', and 7' tall, comprised a two-by-four wood framework, T1-11 plywood siding panels, and a composite shingle roof at a slight angle for runoff over the back rail. These shacks, along with two gang boxes and tool cabinets for each crew, plus the paint department's two huge stationary sand pots near mid-span, all made for quite the cluttered West Sidewalk.

I imagine my shack had sheltered many painters before me. I don't know exactly when the painters' shacks had been built, but upon entering my shack for the first time I noticed the worn olive-brown carpeting on its floor, presumedly installed in the early 70s when shag was groovy.

Our workday started at 7:00 a.m.. All painters were expected to be out of the locker room, in our scooters, and out of the lot no later than 7:05 a.m.. As the South Tower crew, we presided over the shacks located just north of the South Tower.

Every morning from 7:00 a.m. to 8:00 a.m., all journeymen Bridge painters could be found in their shacks, however accommodating the weather may have been. Then, every afternoon we'd be back in our shacks from about 2:15 p.m. to 3:00 p.m. (staying hidden in the tower during these times was also an acceptable practice, but most preferred the shacks). At 3:00, we would all pile into our scooters and head back to the yard. Bridge Management did not want painters to start cleaning up until 3:10, so after our hour of private leisure, we returned to the shop to finish out our day. No veteran painter could even remember when this shack routine had been different. This was more than a tradition; it was a culture.

Not wanting to flaunt the use of our shacks, we would park our scooters at the tower to at least give the impression we might be somewhere working. Of course, other Bridge workers knew better, especially the tradesmen who had good reason to despise us. For them, starting work early each morning right next to the shacks, knowing painters were relaxing inside, sometimes for hours at a time, must have been hard to endure. Imagine ironworkers perhaps hanging a swing stage over the side rail or a basket from above, smelling popcorn cooking in a nearby shack! Or a bridge carpenter repairing a paint shack roof in the rain, all while a couple of painters sat in that shack, dry as a bone, with a space heater, watching the weather report on the television.

While the Bridge workers were not fooled by our performance, the public still needed to be. We kept up the illusion of work by parking our scooters at the tower and walking to our shacks, hoping the motorists who paid premium Bridge tolls would not think their money was going to lounging painters.

I learned quickly the paint shacks were not what they seemed, and did not at all serve the purpose for which they were created. The shacks were an expected privilege enjoyed by self-governed painters. A perk with no conditions attached. An unwritten law that did not need to be rationalized.

The morality issues surrounding this work custom would cause me a lot of doubt over the next couple of years. I began practicing open-mindedness, justifying my own behavior by recalling how it used to be as a painter expected to actually work for the eight hours he got paid. In order to sleep at night, I told myself, "Management is paying me to do this, so it must be the right thing to do."

As a newcomer, I could sense the Paint Department lacked self-awareness in regards to some of our old ways. I can't recall any painters ever truly expressing misgivings about the shacks, not even those who were hard working skilled leaders in the trade. I mean, who wouldn't take advantage of a job benefit like this? So, I shook off my moral qualms about it and continued alongside my crew.

The shacks were meant for journeymen Bridge painters only. Crew foremen were usually busy doing "boss stuff" during our shack times. The apprentices and paint laborers were expected to prepare paint and equipment for us in the morning and clean up after us in the afternoon while we were tucked away in our shacks.

Each shack was small and built to accommodate only two painters. Some shacks had insulated walls, but ours was the roughest, most rudimentary shack I had seen on the Bridge. There was a shag carpet on both the floor and the bench. When we entered the shack, the incoming outdoor breeze would stir the otherwise dormant mixture of dust, sand, and ancient carpet fibers which lifted from the filthy carpet, swirling through the little room with no apparent destination other than right into your open mouth and nostrils.

Our shack came furnished with a bench, a table, and a few shelves. A simple wooden desk was attached to the front wall, situated about a foot above the bench, so you could sit with your legs under it. The desk was home to our hard hats, a couple of old newspapers, and whatever else could be thrown in the garbage by the end of each day. Above the desk were little cubby shelves which stored maybe a flashlight, some spare batteries, ear plugs, pencils, and some old spray gun parts and fittings.

Early on, I found a pile of Polaroid photos stashed in one cubby. These were photos that were taken about ten years earlier, featuring not only painters who had since retired but also those who still worked on the Bridge looking much younger. These photos seemed a bit ominous to me because they showed painters smiling and full of life, painters who now appeared to be physically and mentally worn. An uneasy feeling came over me as I wondered whether it was only natural aging or their years spent on the Bridge that did this to them.

On days the sun was not shielded by clouds or fog, light came in from a sliding window in the back of our shack that faced out toward the sea. This was the only window we could leave uncovered because nobody could see in through it. Each end of the shack had a small plexiglass window that we kept covered. There was also a 12" × 18" window in the front that was also kept covered most of the time, but permanently covering it would have taken away our only way of looking out at the Bridge. Sometimes, we wanted to check the weather or just watch tourists on the sidewalk across the roadway or the cars stopped in traffic, which were only ten feet away from us when we were in our shacks.

To accommodate our need for a versatile front window, my understanding wife sent me to work one day with the only addition we would ever make to our shack: a brass rod, with some little homemade *fleur-de-lis* patterned curtains attached. I could not believe I was bringing them to work intending to install them, but I did, and they were very handy. It was one way to keep those driving by from knowing whether our shack was occupied. Every day when we left the shack, one of us would make sure to shut the curtains. What was I becoming?

The door to the shack could not be on a hinge because opening it outward would put it directly in the path of passing scooters. Instead, a wooden track door was installed. You could slowly ease the door open and make sure all was clear before you exited. The sliding door gave us a further advantage. Upon leaving the shack, we padlocked a latch on the outside of the door. Obviously, if the door was not padlocked, then there were probably painters inside. However, our shack door had an ingenious invention, made from a steel pin about the size of a middle finger, with holes drilled in each end, that you could hang a padlock on. When slipped through a hole in the door, it gave the appearance that the door was locked on the outside and the shack unoccupied, even when painters were inside. A sly subterfuge that was very effective!

The best thing any of our crew's shacks could boast was a battery operated 3" portable TV and a transistor radio. I never thought about how spartan our shack was until I saw some of the other crew's shacks. Most painters regarded their shacks as private spaces, but I could occasionally peek into some of those belonging to veteran painters. Wow! Some were essentially customized living spaces, and it was amazing what they had done within one 8" × 4" lair. *Architectural Digest* could have done a spread on some of the more extravagant shacks I saw. These painters had long since overcome any discomfort they may have had about improper use of the shacks.

There was no electricity in the shacks themselves, but painters conquered this minor obstacle by tapping into the sidewalk light poles. One shack had plush carpet, gorgeous comfortable throw pillows on the soft cushioned bench, and a 19" flat screen TV and DVD player mounted in an upper corner. Also in this corner was a microwave and a little cupboard full of food under the desk. Painters filled the walls with photos of their family as well as pictures of scantily clad girls I suspect were not family members. It was a man cave, a bachelor pad, a primal retreat. The only thing missing was a dartboard and a fully stocked bar that folded out from the wall. No doubt, both had been considered.

Questions crowded my mind when I saw this shack. Are there still fancier ones than this? Could these painters ever move on to a normal painting job after this? Could I? This type of indulgence can't possibly last forever. Cool, is that *Gladiator* you're watching? Scoot over and pass the popcorn.

I heard a story about a painter and his shack that occurred about a year before I began working at the Bridge. Estranged from his girlfriend, he took up temporary residence in his paint shack. The man lived there for three months. He had a space heater, a TV, and some food stocked in his shack. He even claimed he had pizzas delivered to the Toll Plaza in the evenings and would take a scooter across the Bridge to pick up the pizza from the delivery person and bring it back with him. Pizza may not have been the only thing he took back with him. It was said his shack would reek of cheap perfume some mornings.

It was now time to be reacquainted with my new shack mate. He was a middle-aged man known as "Smokey" whom I'd met several times during my years as a painter at Caltrans. Smokey had worked at Caltrans for 34 years before coming to the Golden Gate. He had only been there a year when I started but had already built up an infamous reputation. He would work another ten years with me at the Bridge, and by the time he retired in 2013, at age 65, his legend had grown to monumental proportions.

Drama always seemed to surround Smokey. Most of it did not reflect well on him, but that never bothered him much. Whether it was positive or negative attention, it never mattered, as long as he was getting attention. He was self-centered, a poor listener, and his attempts at humor were often more foolish than funny due to a lack of social perception. Count on him to interrupt any conversation or interject something about himself though what he said bore no relationship to the subject being discussed. Strangely, he seemed to enjoy a joke directed at him. It gave him the chance to occupy center stage. He and I would spend much time antagonizing each other over the years. Highlighted by epic clashes, the two years we spent together in the shack was more than enough time for us to master the art of pissing each other off.

One of his tactics was to come into the confines of the little shack with some sort of horrible smelly food every morning. He would reach into his pocket, pull out a baggie full of meat, and generously offer some to me by quickly opening the bag as close to my face as he could, making sure I got a huge whiff of the mystery meat inside. I would turn away disgusted and spend the rest of the morning half-nauseated in that rank-smelling room.

Smokey knew I preferred to lie on the bench and doze during our morning hour in the shack. He, being wide awake and unable to be still or quiet, didn't want me going to sleep and leaving him without an audience. He would start by reading the newspaper out loud, and no matter how desperately I begged him to stop, he would not. I would finally have to grab the paper from him and wad it up. Every day… same routine!

Then once I got comfortable again, he'd sing some song he had made up himself, usually about Jesus. I would plea with him to stop singing and let me rest. "Why Bob, don't you like Jesus?" might have been one of his sarcastic responses. It was a battle he would win every morning. By the time 8:00 rolled around, I was flustered and impatient to start working, just to get away from him. The mornings belonged to Smokey.

Afternoons, at least, were all mine. When we would get back to the shack at about 2:15, I couldn't stop tapping my feet, waiting to be off work. Smokey, on the other hand, would be tired from the day's work and wanting to rest up for the bicycle ride he took every evening. But this wouldn't happen if I could help it. Every afternoon he would lay on his back the floor of the shack. The moment he fell asleep, I would cover him in a hail of spent sunflower seeds, then maybe locate the crumpled-up newspaper from the morning and throw it in his face. "Get up Bozo, there's no way I'm going to let you sleep after the hell you put me through every morning."

My cheeks hurt from smiling recalling a rare time I bested Smokey. One afternoon, another crew member and I waited for him to doze off, then staple gunned the coveralls he was wearing to the shack floor so he couldn't get up and left him there yelling as we pretended to lock him in the shack. We started the scooter, letting him think we were leaving him stuck there. Oh, how tempting it was to actually do it! As hard as it is to believe, I find myself missing those tumultuous years spent with Smokey in our shack.

Many mornings as I walked out of my shack, the traffic would back up at the Toll Plaza, and I could see slow going on the Bridge. Our shacks were only ten feet from the Number One Lane Southbound. A twinge of guilt grew each time I tried to imagine what a tourist family or morning commuters must have thought as they sat and watched the doors of shacks opening, all up and down the sidewalk, dozens of painters emerging with work boots untied, eating cinnamon buns, and wiping the sleep out of their eyes.

In the afternoon, it looked even more ridiculous: tourists walking or driving across the Bridge, perhaps hoping to get a glimpse of a legendary Golden Gate Bridge painter working up on the main cable or painting the support cables 300 feet above the deck in a basket. Instead, they saw nothing more than a group of well-rested guys meandering out of these cozy shacks on a nice day.

I can readily imagine a family of tourists watching us leave our shacks. "Daddy, look, there's a painter coming out of that little house. Daddy, why does he look like he just woke up? Why is he in his socks? Daddy, what's he doing off the side of the bridge?"

One afternoon, three weeks after starting at the Bridge, I was by myself in the shack and feeling ready to overcome my fear of sleeping at my new job. I had just fallen asleep when I was suddenly awoken by noise and activity outside the shack door. Peeking through the little window, I saw the Paint Superintendent, Rocky. He must have known someone was in there. My heart raced suddenly in my chest, and I jumped up off the bench I was laying on. Was I in trouble? Was this whole sleeping-in-the-shack thing just one big ruse they pull on the new guy?

I finally got up the nerve to crack the door and timidly said, "Hey, Rocky."

He looked over at me, smiled, and said, "Hey, Bob, sorry to bother you. I was just putting reflector tape on the corner of your shack, so the scooters can see the shack when it's foggy or overcast." Then, he added, "I'm done, so get back to whatever you were doing. By the way, how do you like working here so far?"

"How do I like it? How do I like it? Oh, my God, it's the most fabulous job ever!" is what I felt like saying, but still unnerved by the scare, I think I mumbled something cheesy like, "Umm, gosh, I really like it."

Then I shut the door and sank back onto the bench, too wound up to sleep again. I thought to myself, "This really is the best job in the world; my boss basically just caught me sleeping on the job, apologized, and tucked me back into bed!"

After two years at the Bridge, I had gotten used to the shacks, and like all other Golden Gate Bridge painters before me, no longer viewed them as a privilege, but as the norm. However, it is said all good things must end, and the shacks were no different.

Many other tradesmen on the Bridge were so fed up with our shack behavior their jealousy was finally getting the better of them. This had become an interdepartmental issue. The Department Superintendents for both Bridge Management and the ironworkers were now on a mission to have our paint shacks removed from the Bridge. A campaign was started to inform Bridge Management the shacks were just a place where painters went during the workday to sleep and waste time, even on days when the weather was fine for painting.

One afternoon, members of Bridge Management received a tip from other tradesmen about painters sleeping on the job. That same day, they raided some hideaway areas in the towers being used by painters and caught some painters asleep.

This immediately became a big deal. It was a huge embarrassment to the Paint Department, and as punishment, it was determined the shacks would be removed from the Bridge. It was a time of frustration and mourning for the Paint Department. Fingers were pointed at those caught sleeping. Arguments ensued, and fights broke out. The entire department was in turmoil, yet there was still very little accountability concerning what had happened. Nobody mentioned that maybe most, or all, of the blame rested on the painters, and we should consider a concession if we were to save this tradition.

We desperately tried to save the shacks. In our argument, we emphasized the legitimacy of the shacks, the reasons we had long since forgotten and arrogantly abandoned. What about unsafe weather conditions? Or waiting on the ironworkers or for the fog to lift? But it was too late; the die was cast.

Within two days, preparations for removal of the shacks had been made. All belongings were cleared out, including the only personal addition to our shack, the little curtains my wife had made. Though Smokey and I had few items to move out, others were forced to give up a long sacred tradition of the Golden Gate Bridge painters. Their freedom had been taken, or carelessly lost depending on how one looked at it.

Several of us were riding in the commuter van the following Monday when we saw a Southbound Number One Lane closure. The van went silent as we caught sight of a huge crane boom in the blocked-off lane, loading all our shacks, one by one, onto the back of a flatbed semi-trailer. The Ironworker Superintendent was overseeing the crane operation, and the Maintenance Superintendent guided the shacks onto the trailer. The smiles on their faces told the story: they had won. The Bridge's third superintendent, Rocky, was in the commuter van with us, powerless to stop what was happening. He just sat silently staring out the window, humbled as the rest of us. It was a very ignominious moment for the Paint Department.

The Paint Department had lost, but to what extent, I did not know. Sure, a tradition had ended, and this would signal the beginning of the end for a lot of our inherited job perks. But the Golden Gate painters were resilient, and too arrogant to be subdued that easily. Besides, there were plenty of other places for painters to hide from the elements without being discovered, and the removal of the shacks actually served to remind us we needed to be more careful if we were going to continue our shirking.

For me, the elimination of the shacks was not the end of the world. I never really was comfortable lounging in the shacks, and with a shack mate like Smokey, I didn't always enjoy my time there, anyway.

As we were heading home in the van that Monday afternoon, I couldn't help but notice the sudden absence of orange clutter on the West Sidewalk. The eyesores were gone, restoring the Bridge to its former loveliness. The view from the deck, now unobstructed from the West Sidewalk all the way to the horizon, was as beautiful as it was meant to be.

CHAPTER 4

CONDOS

South Tower entrance on the west sidewalk as it veers around the tower

A VIEW THROUGH THE FOG

I will never forget the fateful day the shacks came down. However, the Bridge painters had invented other ways to conceal themselves while they weren't working. Inside the west leg of the South Tower there is a 700-foot-high shaft, identical to the shaft in the east leg, but with no elevator. Tucked discreetly into this tower at roadway level was a nice little hideaway area that had existed many years. After entering through the tower's main security door at the roadway, you veered left through an open hatch. These hatches, found throughout the tower, were circular openings in the floor or wall that were smaller than the passageway itself. Climbing 15 feet up a steel ladder in the very low light, if you glanced to the side, you might have noticed an inconspicuous, well-disguised shelter. Upon closer examination, you may have even noticed that there were actually three of these hideaways, stacked one on top of another. They reminded me of little condos, so from now on, let us call them "the condos."

Many condos like these have existed for decades. While painting, we would occasionally run across one hidden so deep in a tower that it had lain undisturbed and undetected for many years. In these abandoned lairs, you could discover old relics: maybe an old newspaper or rusty tools that belonged to some past worker, but most likely you would just find a pile of really horrible, smelly bedding.

Most painters had their own condos. Some had inherited theirs from retiring painters, and others had created their own. Each condo was about 4' in height and the perfect width and length for a twin-sized mattress. They each had only one entrance, draped with a thick vinyl tarp, to disguise the opening. To enter, you just pulled the flap back and climbed in from the ladder. When the tarp flap was shut, it was the color of the surrounding walls, so in the dim light, it could easily be mistaken for a solid wall.

One particular condo had a twin mattress, a couple of blankets, and a lovely soft pillow. The ceiling was a sheet of plywood, doubling as a floor for the condo above. A drop light hung from the ceiling. A layer of bubble wrap covered the steel walls, working as a comfortable barrier, an insulator for the cold steel in winter, and a noise muffler. There were always mysterious noises and eerie sounds echoing through the towers caused by the creaking of the steel and the howling of the wind.

In one corner was a shelf, just big enough to hold a hard hat, a battery-operated alarm clock, and a few magazines. Running electrical cords was never a problem for those who wanted a portable heater. This was definitely a comfortable place to relax when work slowed, and it was relatively secure from detection because anyone looking up from the bottom of the ladder, would have no idea these holes existed.

Most condos were built in open shafts throughout the towers and had a cleverly constructed framework. The ideal spots to set up these condos were areas with riveted steel walls that were 4'-5' apart and had ladder access close by.

Begin with steel threaded pipes with a 1½- inch diameter and 4" shorter than the distance you are trying to span. Then, screw metal sleeve couplers onto each end of the pipes until you have about an inch clearance on both ends when held between the two walls you are spanning. Next, find a rivet on the wall and then another one on the wall straight across from it. Position the sleeve snugly around one of the rivets, then raise the pipe next to the corresponding rivet on the opposite wall. After that, loosen the sleeves until they fit snugly over the rivets by just turning the pipe in place. Last, securely tighten the pipe up to the steel wall and the sleeves around the rivets to keep the pipe from ever slipping. Four or five of these pipes spaced laterally a foot or so away from each other in a straight line gives you a secure frame in an area that had been only an open shaft before.

Following this, install a sheet of custom-cut marine plywood over the pipes, giving you a secure floor. Now, working off that floor, repeat the piping process 4' above and your ceiling becomes the next floor. Continue on up until you had as many condos as you needed. This area of the South Tower had three condos, but there was an area in the North Tower that had six stacked on each other!

Each crew had its own preferred hangout spots on the Bridge. Painters, of course, knew where other crews' paint shacks were since they were littered across the West Sidewalk, but the condos could be a painter's own secret place. An unwritten rule of respect was that you did not concern yourself with another painter's hiding spot. You knew they existed, and that was all you needed to know.

Apprentices and paint laborers rotate crews, so we could never keep the locations of these hiding areas a total secret. Mike was our crew's apprentice and my work partner, so through the information he shared, I got the skinny on other crew hideouts. I loved to hear the comical stories about the 6-story condos set up in the West leg at the North Tower roadway. One tale concerned a North Tower crew prankster who was always looking for ways to initiate new members into his crew. One of his favorite antics was to wait until the new painter was asleep in his condo, then quietly climb down the ladder until he reached the condo. Completely naked, this joker would sneak into the dark hole, slip in next to the unsuspecting greenhorn, and wake the guy up. The astonished half-awake painter would bolt upright, realize he was lying next to a naked man, and scream, trying to push the naked painter away. The audience of other painters would start whistling and hollering, maybe even taking pictures of the incident, and then the red-faced painter would finally realize he had been hazed. We would subject the rookie painter to good-natured badgering for a long time afterward. When I asked past victims about encounters of this sort, some were good sports about it while others saw no humor in the prank. I am guessing they were careful about where they chose to relax in the future.

Other Departments had heavily scrutinized our shacks. We knew the ironworkers had not only been monitoring our shack use but were also watching us tuck ourselves into our hidden condos. Rumors emerged that Bridge Management had gotten word about the condos. In response, Rocky warned all painters to be more discreet in our use of the shacks and to absolutely avoid any hideaway spots in the towers. Sound advice, but would we listen? Did we ever listen?

The comfortable condo I described earlier belonged to my partner, Mike. I knew this condo well. Sometimes, I would borrow Mike's condo to get some time away from Smokey when he was trying my patience in the shack.

One afternoon, Mike was in the tower. I assumed he was in his spot. At about 2:30, I left my shack and walked to the Southwest Tower, where our scooters were parked in stealth. Twenty minutes still remained until we would be heading back into the yard, so I lingered on the sidewalk, leaning on the outer rail to take in the scenery.

Suddenly I smelled fire and realized that smoke engulfed the Marin Headlands. A grass fire had apparently begun at Kirby Cove, a shoreline campground about a quarter mile west of the Bridge on the north side. Smoke had risen to the top of a hill right beside the Bridge at the Northwest Tower. There was no apparent danger, but the smoke had started blowing onto the Bridge. It was nearing commute traffic time, so the smoke would probably affect traffic on the Bridge, causing visibility problems and encouraging rubberneckers. The hillside beside the Bridge was now actually aflame. Fire crews were on it, but the smoke was still thick and blowing across the roadway like a dense bank of dirty fog.

I was still leaning on the outer rail, my eyes locked on what was happening at the other end of the Bridge, when I was approached by two well-dressed men, obviously Bridge Management, or as they were known to us. "White Hats." I had never seen these men before.

While I had no idea who these White Hats were, I knew they were important. I smiled and said something to them about the fire. They were cordial but seemed to have little interest in me or the fire. Both men went directly to the South Tower, entered through the security door, and closed it behind them.

Later that afternoon, I found out that one of these men was the recently hired Bridge Supervisor and Head Architect. This, in a sense, meant that the Golden Gate Bridge was his. A few years later he would become the Golden Gate Bridge District Supervisor, which would make him head of the Golden Gate Bridge, the Golden Gate Ferry, and the Golden Gate Bus Line. a trifecta earning him the unofficial title of "czar of the Golden Gate."

I knew little about the new man at that time except that in his previous position at Caltrans, he was a major player for years and had a reputation as a union-buster. His main aim had been to eliminate employee time-wasting at Caltrans, and from what I had heard, he was very effective at this. Was he hired to do the same at the Golden Gate Bridge? Probably.

Upon hearing his name, I remembered a recent article I had read about him in the *San Francisco Chronicle.* In this article, he certainly seemed excited about his new job at the Bridge. The article highlighted his career and interviewed people who had worked for him in the past. I remember reading that one employee actually said he trusted this man's good judgment so much that he would walk into a live volcano if asked to. When I read it then and reflect upon it now, I think it was a very odd thing to say. Here was blind faith taken to an unconditional extreme.

I did not concern myself too much with this encounter. I knew Mike was still in the tower, but I figured at that hour of the afternoon he was done relaxing and would soon come out. If he was not up, he had no doubt been woken by the steel tower door opening and closing. Since no White Hats could possibly know about our hidden condos, there should not be a problem. So, I turned my attention back to the excitement of the fire still ablaze at the other end of the bridge and assumed that all was well with Mike in the tower. I could not have been more wrong.

After about five minutes, I saw both White Hats leave the tower. Once of them smiled at me, and I smiled back. Then, he headed straight back to the Toll Plaza, still ignoring the fire at the North End.

A moment later, Mike came out of the tower sweating profusely, looking flushed and frustrated, and shouted in my direction, "Who the hell was that?"

"I don't know," I said, "but he seemed very interested in something inside that tower. Why, what happened?"

"He f–– caught me sleeping in the tower!" Mike responded, obviously shaken. "It was like he came straight in, knew exactly where to look, and found me!"

What happened next in the tower is Mike's account. He heard the tower door close but assumed it was another painter coming in. Then. he heard unfamiliar voices at the bottom of the ladder, so to be safe, he turned off his overhead light and remained quietly under his blanket. Lying there, Mike overheard the junior partner say that he was interested in the seismic area and wanted to check it out, but the Bridge Supervisor told him they could look at it later.

(Below Mike's condo was a landing containing several large junction boxes that computed and relayed seismic information about the tower;. To me, this very interesting-looking area was much too high tech for my understanding.) It seemed the Bridge Supervisor was there for one reason only, and it was not for a sightseeing tour.

Mike then heard the supervisor continue on up the ladder but hoped the tarp cover would give the illusion that there was nothing of interest behind the ladder and he would keep climbing. I like to say that there is a rule about surprises: most of them are not good. Next thing Mike knew, the climber stopped in front of his condo, pulled back the tarp, and looked in, his headlamp shining right into Mike's face. Mike froze like a deer in headlights and went totally silent.

He claims he must have looked like a scared little girl, with his blanket pulled up to his chin and his eyes bulging. He may have even screamed "eek" in his shocked state. He remained frozen as the supervisor, never changing his expression, said nothing, closed the tarp flap, climbed back down the ladder, and left the tower. Mike stayed frozen in place for several minutes after that, still stunned, experiencing a sinking feeling in the pit of his stomach.

We arrived at the painters' locker room 15 minutes later to a loud commotion among the painters. We were told that two other White Hats had concurrently raided the North Tower. The North Tower had a secondary door between the tower door and the condos, and luckily it was bolted shut from the inside. The painters who had taken refuge behind it claimed the White Hats kicked the door and yelled for the painters to open it, a request to which the painters did not respond. Try as they might, the two White Hats could not get into the condo area, but I'm sure they knew what was hidden behind that door.

Other painters loitering around the tower claimed that the White Hats on the North End had shown no interest in the fire. either. After their unsuccessful raid, they exited the tower, ignoring the smoke that was beginning to engulf it, jumped into their scooters. and headed straight back to the Toll Plaza, just as our man had done at the South Tower.

Rocky was informed that the Bridge Supervisor wanted to see him first thing in the morning. Rocky was pissed, and he knew this would not be a good meeting. For the rest of the afternoon, the entire Paint Department was in a state of anxiety, a steady stream of "blame bombs" being thrown from crew to crew. The true magnitude of the raid was not realized until the next morning when the main instigator of the ambuscade, none other than the new Bridge Supervisor himself, informed Rocky that his incriminating discoveries resulted from a "random routine inspection" of the towers and that he was very disappointed in what he'd found. A "random routine inspection." Really? Whatever it was, the White Hats obviously knew that there were painters lounging in the towers, and the sheer coincidence that a fire was raging on the North End did not deter them from their mission to expose us.

The whole incident reminded me of an old black-and-white episode of *The Untouchables* where the incorruptible Eliot Ness arrives with his G-men, holding an axe, ready to raid Frank Nitti's liquor stash while his associates prepare to kick down doors at all the gangs' other hideouts simultaneously. Nothing would get in his way.

The result of that crazy afternoon was not only the removal of all the paint shacks on the West Sidewalk, as described earlier, but also the elimination of any condos that were known to exist. The painters were dug in deep, and they could not root out all our spots, but this was definitely the beginning of the end of our Paint Department's cultural departure from acceptable work ethics.

Mike took most of the blame for the loss of the shacks, but we were going to lose them one way or the other. The powers that be were just too determined, and we were too careless… and c'mon, should anyone really get to enjoy their job as much as we did?

My first encounter with the new Bridge Supervisor had left me with more questions than answers. Was he someone who had so little concern for his Bridge that he could ignore the threat of a fire, or was he a righteous enforcer dedicated to rooting out laziness in the workplace? Either way, he had made a tremendous impact early in his reign.

I kept thinking about that article I'd read a few days before. I wondered if one of the henchmen who entered the North Tower amid a spreading fire was the same man who had claimed he would walk into a live volcano if he'd been asked to. If so, then how very apropos.

The Supervisor and his loyal volcano walkers had won today, but…

CHAPTER 5

SCOOTERS

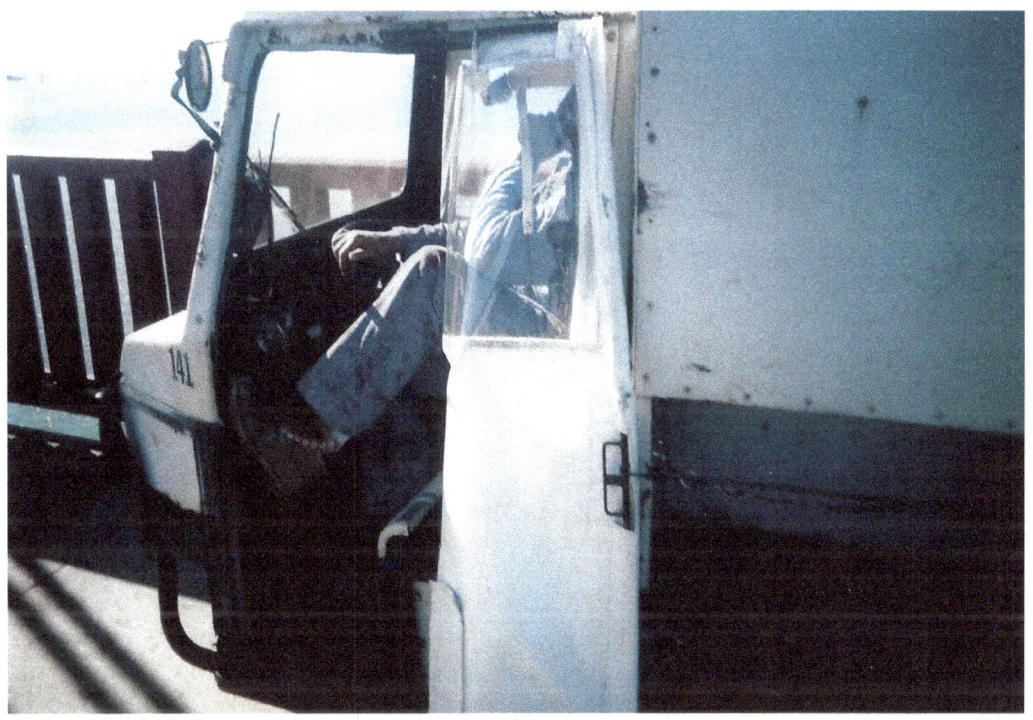

Scooter 141: one of our crew's Cushman bridge scooters. We ran these scooters hard, until they finally needed to be replaced by the less practical Biagi scooters.

A VIEW THROUGH THE FOG

Scooters were our primary means of transportation up and down the sidewalks of the Bridge. We used Cushman scooters when I was first starting out, but these scooters had been run hard over the years and were eventually replaced by new Biagi scooters from Italy. Each scooter had a utility box built onto its back for transporting crew members and supplies. This steel compartment was 6' × 4' and about 5' feet tall. Inside was a pair of fold-up bench seats covered with vinyl cushions. A metal bar overhead held our harnesses, lanyard hooks, and ropes and functioned as a handle for those riding in the back. Once inside, you banged on the side of the scooter with your hand so the driver knew to proceed or stop.

The cab was very small. The scooters had manual transmissions, so the driver crammed into this tiny space had a hard time operating the clutch, especially when another rider was in the cab, taking up elbow room.

The Cushmans were old and beaten, and the original doors had been torn off many years earlier. The makeshift doors had vinyl covers attached to thin steel-rod frames and were usually tied back open except on cold or rainy days. These doors were ripped off regularly. I bet that every painter, whether or not willing to admit it, has caused a scooter door being torn off at least once, either by clipping a shack, a rail, or even another scooter. In fact, a gust of wind can blow a scooter door open so hard that the frame bends. The Bridge mechanics were forever replacing them. Our crew was notorious for destroying scooter doors, and Mike had damaged so many that another crew member who tore a door off could blame it on Mike without question.

The Cushmans were gas operated with 3-speed transmissions. They had governors installed to limit speed because the last thing the Bridge needed was for painters or ironworkers to drive dangerously and injure tourists or themselves. You could get your scooter to a top speed of 18 MPH, but if you had a speed demon on your crew like Mike, who could manipulate the downward grades and straights, there was a possibility of getting the scooter up to 22 MPH on the West Sidewalk.

On the East Sidewalk, speeding was never an issue because there was always a lot of bicycles and foot traffic, and you spent most of your ride pushing the horn, warning tourists and bicyclists of your presence, and either waiting on or dodging them. Sometimes. the quarter mile from the South Tower to the Toll Plaza could take 15 minutes in a scooter.

Each paint crew typically had three scooters: two paint scooters and a foreman scooter. Our Foreman hated giving rides to other painters on the crew, so he kept his cab cluttered and always filled the back of his scooter with wet paint buckets and open thinner cans. This method was so effective that when one of our scooters was down for repair, we preferred to pack seven painters like sardines into one scooter rather than ride in his "hazardous-waste-mobile."

Our crew shared two scooters. Stew and Robin rode in the cab of scooter #170 with Smokey in the back. Scooter #141 had Kevin and Junior in front while Mike and I rode in back. Why Kevin and Junior rode in the front I will never know because Kevin was 6'5" and Junior was an inch shorter. With their long legs, they could barely fit in the cab, let alone shift and brake the vehicle, which may explain why riding with them reminded me of being at Disneyland on Mr. Toad's Wild Ride.

A variety of other scooters roamed the sidewalks. There were scooters with crew boxes, flatbed scooters, and little tow scooters equipped with winches to tow their disabled counterparts. Some had mounted fuel tanks while others, called "water buffalos," carried tanks for water. One type of scooter our crew used was called a "mule," meant for hauling sand. It had a full-sized diesel engine and a mass of concrete and steel in its rear end to help balance its load when transporting our sand trailers across the West Sidewalk.

Another type of scooter belonged to the Bridge Patrol. This little paddy-wagon vehicle was even smaller and shorter than the regular scooters, less than 5' tall, with barely room for a driver and passenger in front. A woven wire partition separated the cab area from a small area in back with two narrow bench seats. There was a rear hatch, allowing passengers or detainees to squeeze into the back. The Bridge Patrol scooters were even painted black and white, like real police vehicles.

The Paint Department had turned one of these tiny scooters into a back-up paint scooter. It was repainted solid white and used when one of our scooters was being borrowed or repaired. It seemed like our crew always got stuck with that scooter. I think someone must have thought it was funny to make the crew with the tallest painters use the tiniest vehicle. By packing six good-sized painters into this little scooter, you could expect to get quite the looks and laughs from tourists and other painters as we exited the back hatch one after another. This was as close to a circus clown car as you could imagine.

One situation in particular may illustrate what I mean. Our crew was working at the South Tower, using this little white ex-security scooter. Junior pulled the scooter in front of the tower to let us all out. Some of a large group of Japanese tourists nearby started hovering around our scooter when the back hatch sprang open. We began squeezing out of the back, one by one, as the tourists smiled and took pictures. We were looking around at each other, wondering what was going on. The last to exit was Smokey. The group of tourists had now grown to about a dozen, and as he stepped out of the scooter, the group began to clap and cheer. Not having any idea why the tourists were cheering, but enjoying the attention, Smokey raised his hand triumphantly and yelled, "Yeah!" Then, he looked at me and whispered, "Why are they cheering?"

I answered, "I don't know for sure, but I think they believe this is some sort of performance we're putting on."

"What kind of performance?"

"Like clowns in a circus who all pile out of a clown car, I guess. I don't know!"

"Huh?" Smokey, still confused, had no clue what I was talking about. He looked back at the smiling tourists, held both his hands up, and yelled even louder, "Yeah!"

Imitating him, the crowd raised their hands up and returned a yell, "Yeah!"

Then, we all stepped into the tower, laughing. The last one in, Smokey gave one final "Yeah!" to the crowd before shutting the door behind him.

We could hear the tourists outside the door respond with one more exuberant "Yeah!"

Shaking my head as he shut the door, I smiled and said to him, "Dude, you really are a clown, but you sure can work a crowd!"

Some scooters had swing doors on the back for privacy. They were made of plexiglass and sometimes painted with unique designs. One set of doors had a big smiley face and another a huge depiction of a martini glass. Our crew's scooters had no design because we had no back doors. It was our Foreman's belief that they led other Bridge workers to assume there was sleeping going on back there, so we removed ours.

Actually, our scooter boasted something much more noticeable. Kevin and Junior had attached a set of real deer antlers to the front of each side of the scooter. They looked obnoxious, but our "deer scooter" was a real crowd-pleaser. We rode around with these antlers protruding from the scooter for a couple of years. Finally, Management asked us to remove them. I was pretty surprised that the antlers lasted as long as they did, and the fact we did not impale somebody or poke a tourist's eye out on the sidewalk was remarkable.

Scooter horseplay was always going on. For example, you could not drive your scooter past the North Tower crew early in the morning without someone throwing a cup of ice water through your scooter door and into your face. Nor could you drive past them without worrying that they might rope-hook your bumper as you passed, causing your scooter to abruptly stop and sometimes actually ripping your rear bumper off.

Another scooter prank would involve tying a tire on a rim to a rope and hooking it to a bumper as the driver took off through the parking area. The wheel would start bouncing and hopping wildly behind the scooter. We were lucky that these out-of-control wheels killed no one. Eventually, this antic was stopped when one of the wheels smashed into a district truck and destroyed its door. The maintenance superintendent was not pleased, and the next day *Rules of Scooter Conduct* were implemented. Of course, tying things to scooter bumpers was declared a big no-no and could result in termination.

Our crew was blamed for the tire incident even though the North Tower painters were actually the ones who hooked the tire to our bumper, so retaliation was inevitable. While all the painters were on break one morning, Junior spent the entire 30 minutes stacking blocks underneath the North Tower crew scooter, raising it just far enough that each wheel was about an inch off the ground. When the break ended. the North Tower crew piled into its scooter, started it up, and put it in gear, but the scooter would not move. A crowd of painters and ironworkers gathered around, and, of course, we could all see its little wheels turning forward, then backward, then forward again.

Mark, the driver, yelled out the scooter window, "The transmission is shot."

Junior replied, "Yep, transmission's shot. Hey, rev the engine once more real high; it sounds like it's catching."

Mark laid into the gas, and we all laughed as the wheels spun even faster. Junior finally pointed down to the wheels, and Mark leaned out the window to look. He saw the blocks, then looked at Junior, shut the motor off, sank back into his seat, and put his head down in shame. The crowd around the scooter laughed and cheered while Junior bowed to them. Sweet retribution!

One time, our crew was down a scooter, and we had to borrow Rocky's. Superintendents used special electric scooters. The cabs of these scooters were veiled only in vinyl material and had soft plastic windows, leaving virtually no protection, but how protected do you need to be in a scooter traveling only 10 MPH on a sidewalk?

This scooter belonged to the boss, so discretion should definitely be exercised when driving this vehicle, right? Well, tell that to my partner Mike, who had an addiction to driving fast, whether it be cars, motorcycles, boats, bicycles, or scooters. As I mentioned, he prided himself on getting the most speed possible out of a scooter.

The boss' scooter had a 4-speed transmission and no governor to limit its speed. We were bringing it back from the North End one afternoon when Mike decided that he just could not resist testing the speed of this scooter. After careening around the South Tower and gathering momentum the last stretch of the West Sidewalk, Mike reached a top speed of 51 MPH. Now, I had never been over 22 MPH in a scooter (even that was excessively fast), so this seemed like Mach speed to me. I was holding on for my life.

I noticed we were actually passing cars speeding down the Bridge roadway, and I could see their occupants looking over at us like we were crazy as we barreled past them. Mike *was* crazy. I could see it in his eyes. I was crazy, too, for getting in this scooter with him, but none of that would matter if we crashed and died.

I realized we were coming up fast on a part of the sidewalk that narrows at the anchor block, between the concrete wall and the guardrail, to a width that is hard to fit through when going 5 MPH, let alone the 50 MPH we were approaching it at.

I believed my life was in danger because running into a concrete block head-on at that speed in a vinyl scooter would not be good. Mike began braking, and the scooter rocked from side to side, unable to stay straight. We skidded through the narrow opening at over 30 MPH, just missing the concrete block, glancing off the safety rail and then the inner block wall before coasting to a stop.

The two of us stared straight ahead, both panting and sweating. All I managed to say was, "Whew, let's see someone else try to take a scooter faster than that!"

Mike looked at me and said, "I will…tomorrow."

I laughed. "Then tomorrow may be a good day for me to take off!" I never got into that scooter with him again.

Scooter accidents were not unheard of, and two stand out in my memory. One occurred at the North End approach while we were sandblasting underneath. Our crew trailers were set up below, and scooters would make their way down a dirt road and then take a slight incline to reach them. We were relaxing in our trailer when we heard a loud crash right outside the door. We had no idea what had happened until we opened the door to find another crew's scooter lying on its side just outside the trailer. The two riders in the cab were one on top of the other, and as we hurried to help them, three painters came rolling out of the back of the scooter. All riders luckily walked away with only minor injuries. No official cause of the wreck was ever issued, but with a little sleuthing and a lot of gossip, we came to suspect that the wreck was a combination of horseplay in the back of the scooter and excess speed when rounding the corner. Knowing who the riders were, both assumptions were likely accurate.

Another scooter wreck happened one afternoon about a month after I started at the Bridge. It involved both Kevin and Junior. Junior was driving the mule down the sidewalk and Kevin was following behind him in one of our crew's scooters. They were both driving as fast as their vehicles could go, heading back to the Toll Plaza. Junior, ever the wise guy, slammed on the brakes of the mule, with its massive concrete-and-steel backside, Kevin, following too closely, had no time to stop and crashed into the back of the mule so hard that his scooter folded into an inverted "V" upon impact, nearly splitting across the middle. He was thrown against the dash hard enough to fracture a rib, and his head hit on the windshield with enough force to break the glass.

The two of them managed to drag the scooter into the yard, and they just left it there, mentioning nothing about the wreck or Kevin's injuries. The next morning, we all saw the scooter sitting there in a heap and wondered what the heck had happened. but when Kevin came limping into work, it didn't take long to surmise who'd been involved in this wreck.

Later that morning, Kevin admitted to our crew what had happened. The official report stated a Coke bottle had rolled under the brake pedal and he could not stop the scooter in time. The scooter was repaired and put back into service. Kevin's injuries mended in time although his driving rights were suspended.

Eventually, the time came to replace the worn-out Cushman scooters on the Bridge. Maintenance Superintendent Craig was put in charge of restocking our Cushman inventory or else finding a better alternative. He chose Biagi Motors, an Italian company, and Biagi shipped a few demo scooters for us to try. The consensus on the new scooters was not good. They had even less cab space than the cramped Cushmans and thin metal doors with flimsy slide-up glass windows. These demos were also longer than the Cushmans, and we already had a hard enough time turning those around on the Bridge sidewalks as it was.

Still, Craig thought he could overcome any of these problems with modifications, and he got management's blessing to buy a fleet of the Italian scooters. Those of us who worked on the Bridge every day did not understand this decision. It just made no sense to choose these overpriced, over-sized, impractical scooters.

Craig and Archie, the Bridge body and fender specialist, spent the better part of a year modifying these scooters. They removed about a foot from each bed, but even this was not enough to make them capable of turning around on the sidewalks. The new scooters were wider than the Cushmans, leaving just barely enough room for two scooters to pass each other on the narrow sidewalk, with the wheels clipping each other in passing. To prevent the wheels from being destroyed, they installed a special aluminum side bumper over the rear wheels. These modifications were required for every new scooter purchased.

Even then, the scooters still did not measure up to the oldest and most worn of the Cushmans. Any crew who still had one prized it as if it were gold. As time went on, if a Cushman had any type of an operational problem at all, a club was placed on the steering wheel, its crew box was reinstalled on a new Biagi scooter, and the unfortunate Cushman was taken to the Boneyard, dismantled, and put out of commission. Thse scooter transformations had almost a *Frankenstein* feel to them.

The scooters became another daily battleground for Smokey and me. Our crew often worked off the West Sidewalk, underneath the roadway at mid-span. The scooter would stop when it reached our work site. We would hop out of the back, hit the side of the scooter once we had safely exited, and the driver would head on up to the North Tower where he would turn around. Smokey would usually jump out, then reach back in to grab his coat before the scooter would proceed. This coat of his was a silver down jacket, years old, filthy, full of holes, and reeking of old fish. I really hated that coat.

Several times I tied its sleeves around the braces of the seat in the back of the scooter, so when Smokey jumped out and grabbed it, the scooter would take off and he would hold on to the coat just long enough that it would pull him down to the ground before he could let go. I should have been more considerate to the old guy, but hey, I always got a good laugh from the crew, and also, I'm sure he deserved it for some other annoying thing he had done to me that day.

One day, I was feeling extra playful, so I prepared a special surprise for Smokey. I noticed his coat on the floor when we got into the scooter that morning, so during the 5-minute ride to the job site, I carefully attached a hook with a 25-foot rope fastened to it through a hole in the back of his coat. Then, I tied the rope to the seat. Once at the job site, we jumped out, and as soon as Smokey grabbed his coat, I beat on the side of the scooter giving them the signal to move on. The scooter took off, and the rope dropped to the ground and started unraveling. It was all going as planned. The rope would soon pull taut and the coat would be yanked out of Smokey's hand and dragged down the sidewalk behind the scooter. What a grand scheme—or so I thought.

What I did not expect was that Smokey would be so oblivious to what was going on that he actually put an arm into his coat! The driver did not know that a rope was unwinding from back of the scooter, and he built up some speed in those 25 feet. The rope tightened before I had time to say anything, and there went Smokey, pulled to the ground and rolling along for about ten feet, until, thank God, he fell out of his coat. He lay there on his back in the middle of the West Sidewalk, stunned, as his coat flopped away behind the scooter.

The crew all ran over to see if Smokey was all right. They were half-laughing, half-concerned for his well-being. My first thought was that I might have injured the poor old guy, but then I saw him raise his head and was relieved he was at least alive.

A crew member asked, "What the hell happened?"

I answered quickly before Smokey spoke. "I think he accidentally hooked his coat on that rope hook."

Another crew member responded, "Smokey, I told you to get rid of that old nasty coat!"

Smokey spun to look at me, furious. "You a—hole, I know you did that!"

With a devious smile, I replied loudly enough for only Smokey to hear. "I did the crew a service by getting rid of that coat, plus gave them a little entertainment. And they also think your lame butt hooked yourself to that rope…win, win, and win!"

Well, Smokey was okay after the fall, but he kept that horrible coat another year until someone (I wonder who?) finally just threw it off the Bridge.

As I'd mentioned, I usually rode in the back of scooter #141 and Smokey rode in the back of scooter #170. Smokey wore ear plugs all day. He would go through dozens of pairs a week and had a rude habit of just disposing of them anywhere.

I noticed him in the back of our scooter one day taking the ear plugs from his ears and then doing something on our seat with them. After he left, I went to inspect and saw that the seat cushion had a hole in it. I peeled back the vinyl to find a collection of used dirty ear plugs he had been stuffing inside the seat for who knows how long. It was nasty, and I made him pick every one of them out and told him he could do that in his own scooter, not mine.

Well, as expected, he was unfazed and expressed no remorse, so I took it upon myself to dispense my own style of justice. I gathered up an entire bag of half-eaten chicken wings and went to scooter #170, sliced a little hole in the vinyl seat cover where he would normally sit, and started stuffing the cushions with old chicken. Once I'd crammed the entire bag of chicken into his seat, I just had to wait it out. I checked the scooter every day for a week. Nothing. Finally, I just figured that it would happen when it happened, and I was sure he'd let me know when the stink caught up with him.

It was not long after this that the Bridge made the switch from the Cushmans to the new Biagi scooters. After they made the modifications to the new fleet, the crew boxes on the back were transferred over, and our new scooters were ready for use.

The first time I jumped in the back of our new scooter #141, I immediately fell back. What the heck was that smell? Then, I started figuring things out. Archie had put the #170 shell on scooter #141, and vice versa. Frantically, I dropped to inspect the seat and saw the slit I had made. It felt like an episode of *The Twilight Zone*.

"Nooooo!" There it was, all the old chicken I'd shoved in there and some ear plugs Smokey had stuffed on top of that, in *my* scooter. I spent the next hour emptying the chicken and ear plugs, doing my best not to throw up. Then, of course, Smokey came walking by, holding his nose and peering into the scooter, "What is that awful smell?"

I just looked at him wordlessly. There was nothing to say in that moment. Lose, lose, and lose!

A VIEW THROUGH THE FOG

CHAPTER 6

WOMEN JUMP, TOO

Beyond the safety rail, the narrow outer chord gives you very little space to operate and maneuver, even for a bridge worker.

A VIEW THROUGH THE FOG

The occurrence of Bridge suicides is apparently random. Sometimes, there can be three or four jumps in a week, and other times, several months may go by without a reported jump. One fact, not so random, is that male jumps far outnumber female jumps (three males to each female). However, women do unfortunately jump, and when it happens, it makes a permanent impression, very different from seeing a male jump.

It was a rare sunny afternoon at the Bridge, the fog having lifted hours earlier. Mike and I had been assigned the task of attending to the sandblast pots at mid-span on the West Sidewalk. Other crew members sandblasted rust off the underside of the road deck and floor beams directly below us.

As point men for the operation, our principal duties included keeping the sandblast pots filled with sand and coordinating with the crew below using Bridge radios. As the afternoon drew to a close, we shut the operation down and waited for the rest of our crew to climb up from below. Leaning on the outer safety rail, I took a moment to enjoy the gorgeous day, but my reverie was interrupted when I noticed some unusual activity across the roadway about a hundred yards from where we stood.

Number One Lane Northbound, the lane closest to the sidewalk, had been closed off by Bridge patrol. A patrol vehicle had pulled right up behind a car that appeared to be stalled. This was not a rare sight on the Bridge, but curiosity had gotten the best of us. So, Mike and I started down the opposite sidewalk to get a better view.

The vehicle was parked a bit irregularly, with the driver's side door still open, and it looked to be abandoned. A commotion had begun on the East Sidewalk. A small woman stood with her back against the outer guardrail. She appeared to be in an agitated state.

Curious, I turned on my Bridge radio and listened as Bridge security assessed the situation. The report said the woman stopped her vehicle in the first lane, jumped out, ran around the car, crawled through the safety barrier that separates the roadway from the sidewalk, and then ran across the sidewalk to the outer rail where she appeared to be in some sort of stand-off with two Bridge security officers.

I saw the officers cautiously approach the nervous woman, who now had one of her hands on the guardrail, the other at her side. The officers were careful to keep a safe distance and seemed to plead with her. Why not just pounce on her and grab her before she had a chance to jump over the rail? The answer came over the Bridge radio.

According to the report, she held several hypodermic needles in her hand and began acting violently toward the officers. I could see the woman, needles in hand, wielding them like knives, vigorously hacking and slashing at the air. She was remarkably menacing for someone so small. Each time the officers moved closer to her, she poked and jabbed them away. She obviously did not want anyone near her.

Then, as if having no doubts or second thoughts about accomplishing what she had come to the Bridge to do, she rolled her petite frame up and over the guardrail so quickly that the lunging officers had no chance of grabbing her. She left our view. She had jumped. Mike and I gasped in horror. We knew that the only thing beyond the rail was a 3-foot-wide steel chord and then a 200-foot fall to the waters below. Surely, she was gone.

Both officers quickly approached the rail and looked over. Then, a frantic report came over our radio saying that the woman was actually still holding onto the outer edge of the chord. We looked at each other in amazed approval, but no sooner had we gotten our hopes up than we saw the officers twist their bodies in frustration. We knew at that moment, the woman could not hold on any longer or had let go on her own. Either way, she had obviously fallen. By this time, the Coast Guard had positioned themselves below her, but soon after, we heard the radio describing it as a recovery, not a rescue. Grief overwhelmed me. The incident happened so fast!I It is impossible to explain the emotional overload and feeling of futility to witness something like this and be utterly helpless to assist.

I feel sorrow for the two Bridge patrol officers and what they must have to live with, always wondering if they should have just sacrificed themselves and taken a stab from the needles filled with who knows what, to save a woman who wanted more than anything to die on that day.

CHAPTER 7

THE BONEYARD

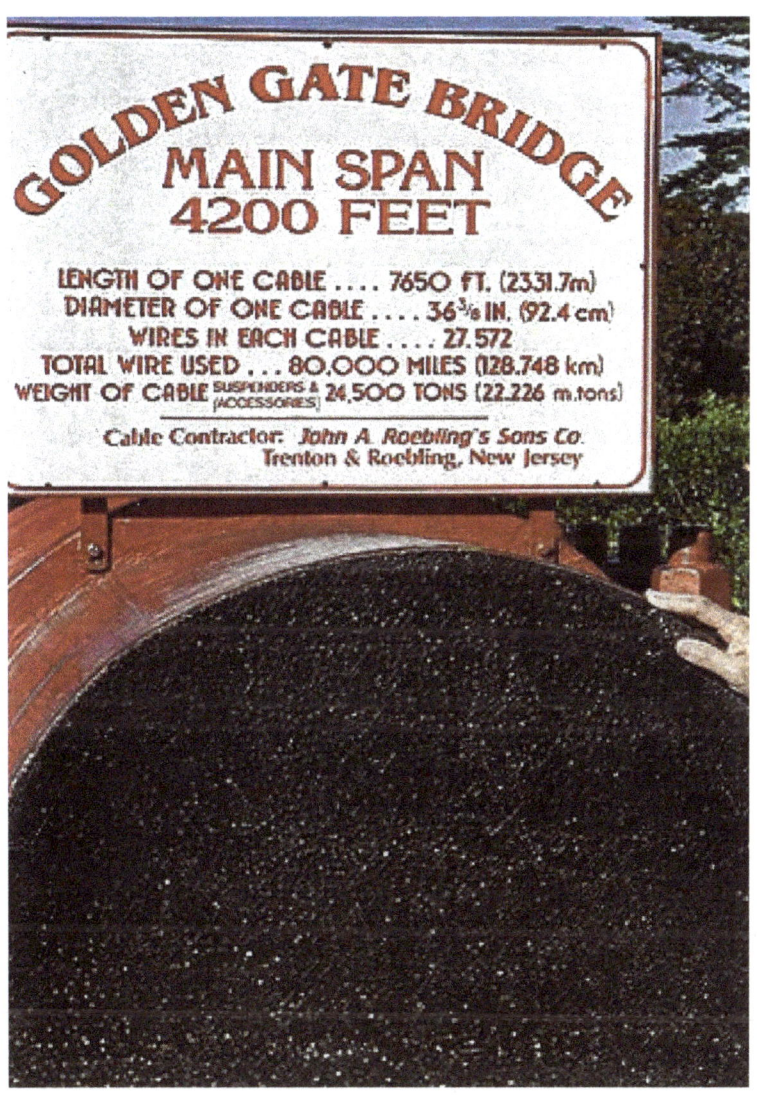

A section of the cables that support the Golden Gate Bridge, along with information about the bridge, displayed near the Boneyard, at the Vista Point South.

A VIEW THROUGH THE FOG

The Boneyard, as it was called, had been established at the San Francisco end of the Golden Gate Bridge, set off from the Toll Plaza just below the east parking lot. It was located at the foot of a small hill and surrounded by trees, hidden from the public. An area at least as old as the Bridge, "Boneyard" had been named, I assumed, for its function as an on-site scrap yard. Besides discarded Bridge items, storage containers, a sandblast booth, a paint shop, a hazardous waste disposal station, several greenhouses used by landscapers, and other minor facilities could be found in the Boneyard.

Among the many relics were miles of suspension cables that had been cut and replaced, paint shacks that had been removed, and a mound of crashed scooters. One might stumble upon outdated toll booths such as the "peanut booths," which could collect tolls from both the driver's side and the passenger's side and had rested in the Boneyard for over 40 years.

Also in the Boneyard heap of memories was a giant clock which had sat atop the Toll Plaza from 1948 until July 23, 2003. What a wonder to see this clock, with its eight-foot diameter face, equipped with neon tubes on both the hands and the numbers, finally taken out of service because of exposure to the salty air over the years! The Boneyard was a museum that no one got to see.

When I started at the Bridge, the Boneyard was an area frequented almost exclusively by the Paint Department. The Boneyard crew was one of five paint crews that made up the Paint Department. Membership was exclusive, and turnover was rare. A spot was usually held until a painter retired. Other paint crews joked that the Boneyard crew was made up of worn-down, aging veterans, and this was where old painters went to die. Truth was, we all would have jumped at the chance to be a member of that crew.

The Boneyard crew never had major jobs on the Bridge. I am not saying they weren't busy; it was just that we rarely ever saw them on the Bridge itself. They did not need to use our locker room, lunchroom, or even our parking lot because they had all these facilities at the Boneyard. Aside from when they signed in and out each day, we saw little of them.

If the Paint Department were a major league baseball team, the Boneyard crew would have been the relief pitchers with their own area set behind the outfield fence where they hung out together all game as a unit, away from the rest of the team in the dugout. They were definitely part of the team, just with a different role to fill, and their overall contribution was very important.

Upon entering the Boneyard, one saw the crew's huge green canvas tent. I jokingly referred to it as the "Winchester Mystery Tent." Briefly glancing around the interior, one got the impression that it was a functional, self-supporting crew facility. There was a fully operational work area; a nice break room with a card table (these guys loved to play cards), a changing area with lockers, and a little office for the crew foreman. The crew was always friendly to me when I entered the tent, but I got the feeling they did not want me examining the place too closely.

Interesting rumors gave the tent a special mystique. It was said that one wall inside this large tent actually concealed strategically placed little anterooms that served the

Boneyard crew with the same benefits that the shacks and condos did for us painters on the Bridge. I never saw these rooms with my own eyes, but thought I could sense their presence when I was there.

Barney was the foreman of the Boneyard paint crew and a man anyone would want to work for. He had an excellent relationship with management, but more important, he knew how the Bridge operated. He was outgoing and had a great sense of humor. Barney was one of those worthy men found in every vocation, universally respected on the Bridge. The difference between a good leader and a bad one is about five heartbeats: good leaders make immediate choices. Barney was a stand-up guy and never one to shrink from hard decisions.

One thing that stood out most about his crew were their genuine smiles. Looking around the crew room at the end of the workday, the painters who looked the most relaxed and content were usually the members of Barney's crew—a result of good leadership. I had worked with bosses in the past who gave their workers complete freedom, but when the workers were caught in compromising situations, they were on their own; those unconcerned bosses often left them to their own demise. This never seemed to be the case with Barney. He backed his men unconditionally, so in turn, they did their best not to let him down. It was an extended family, the basis for a well-oiled machine.

Barney was a plump, jolly looking man, which played into his most memorable role perfectly. Every Christmas Eve, he would come to work dressed as Santa. He would take one of the flatbed scooters, decorate it with Christmas lights, load it with wrapped packages, and then he and his wife (dressed as Santa's elf) would drive the scooter up and down the Bridge sidewalk, waving to all the commuters and tourists. Barney at his best!

Now, I'm not saying Barney was a perfect employee. There may have been some duplicitous reasons his crew had smiles on their faces every day. Rumors always surrounded the Boneyard crew.

The Boneyard's most important function was sandblasting. This was a different type of blasting than what we did on the Bridge and specialized in blasting specific items on a much smaller scale. There was an efficiently contained sandblast booth in the Boneyard with a 5-bag (500 pounds of sand) sand pot. Items that were blasted in the Boneyard might include newly fabricated steel such as lacings or gusset plates, district vehicle body parts, and even items as random as city parking meters or anchors from ferries. The Boneyard blaster would first blast and then immediately zinc-coat prime the items because the Bridge's wet environment would cause the steel to rust within hours of being blasted. These odd jobs were an essential part of the Paint Department's work.

Roger was the Boneyard sandblaster. An outgoing, outspoken, hot-headed painter, he was a guy everyone knew and either loved or hated. He was officially listed as a member of the Boneyard paint crew, but other than showing up for their bi-monthly safety meetings, he worked alone and reported directly to our Paint Superintendent. For all intents and purposes, he was Rocky's right-hand man. Their relationship was not complicated.

He was just a kiss-ass of epic proportions, with no shame in his game. Roger openly embraced this role, and Rocky blatantly used him as such. Roger's excessive brown-nosing and the boss's favoritism appalled some painters but usually only because they wished they were the ones getting the attention. The rest of us just laughed it off and hoped he kept Rocky happy because our lives were certainly easier when the boss was smiling.

I might compare this arrangement between Rocky and Roger to the relationship between a shark and a pilot fish. The shark can eat the little pilot fish at any time he wishes, but why would he? The pilot fish cleans the shark and keeps all the annoying parasites from afflicting him. If the pilot fish does his job, then he has protection against all other predators who wait for him to be alone so they can devour him. A profitable alliance for both.

One morning while most other painters were out working, I went into the lunchroom and found Roger frying bacon and eggs. I asked him what he was doing, and he told me he was cooking the boss breakfast. I told him to make sure he did a good job! Rocky loved chicken, and thanks to Roger, there was a greasy, fragrant bag of chicken left at Rocky's office door almost every day at lunchtime for years.

Because he did so many of Rocky's personal errands, Roger was given a long leash. He had his sandblast job down to a science and never procrastinated. He accomplished his daily tasks quickly and efficiently, making sure the rest of the day was his. Many jealous Bridge employees would have loved to see Roger get caught away from the job, but he was way too crafty for that. We assumed he carried his Bridge Maintenance radio with him even when he was not at the Bridge. Sometimes, we would laugh when a radio call was made for Roger late in the afternoon, wondering if this would be the day he got caught, but he would respond every time. Where he was, who knows. Sometimes, his voice sounded slurred and tired, but he always answered.

Roger was a bachelor in his early 50s when I met him, a guy who seemed very confident with himself as a ladies' man but tired of the chase. A guy who, instead of buying women drinks all night, would rather just show up at last call and take his chances on the girls who remained. No effort was put into his pickup lines, either. I remember riding in a Bridge vehicle to lunch with him one day, a truck that had a big Golden Gate Bridge decal on each door. We were on Lombard Street looking for a place to eat. Roger's window was down, and every time we stopped, he would ask a girl walking by, "Excuse me. Miss, could you tell me where the Golden Gate Bridge is?" Some would see the emblem on the door and giggle. Others would look at him like he was a complete idiot, and some would actually give us directions to the Bridge! I had to wonder which of these three responses was most appealing to him.

I finally looked over at him and said, "Man, that is one horrible line. Stop that, it's embarrassing."

"Quantity over quality, quantity over quality… you only need one to bite," was all he said, smiling.

Staring at him, I shook my head, not even knowing what the hell he was talking about.

Roger had his own shack in the Boneyard, identical to our shacks on the West Sidewalk. Some of the office girls from the Bridge, and even some who worked at the Bridge café, it was said, frequented his shack during many a lunch hour. Girls were rumored to have been seen leaving the shack with messed up hair and smeared lipstick. Once, my curiosity prompted me to look inside his shack when it was unoccupied. It was not very clean and definitely did not look like a babe lair, but he was a favorite with many of the girls at the Bridge, so let's just file these stories of shack romance under "good gossip" and leave it at that.

Roger wore many hats: a ladies' man, a brown nose, a smooth talker, , a good sandblaster. A man like Roger could only have thrived in an environment like the Golden Gate Bridge Paint Department. Will guys like him eventually cease to exist, like dinosaurs, or will there always be a Roger in every workplace?

Another interesting member of the Boneyard crew was known as "The Russian." In all our years of painting together on the Bridge, I was never formally introduced to him, and I never took the time to find out his full name. I doubt he even knew my first name, nor did he care to know it, or most of the other painters' names, for that matter. He seemed totally oblivious to the rest of us. I probably never said more than 20 words to him in all the time we worked together. All his jobs were evidently in the Boneyard because I never saw him on the Bridge. For long periods of time, I would forget he even existed. Then, I'd catch sight of him and say to my partner, "Hey, look, that Russian guy still works here. I thought he retired years ago!"

He was probably in his mid-50s and looked as strong as an ox. He was always squinting through a pair of thick glasses. He was quiet and reserved but seemed like the kind of guy who you did not want mad at you. When he did speak, it was with a heavy Russian accent.

I did hear one sound from him regularly when he showed up at our monthly Paint Department safety meetings. Ten minutes into every meeting, a loud bear-like snore would start drifting from the back of the room. We knew who it was without even turning around and would start giggling among ourselves. Rocky never said a word to him and just continued with the meeting, despite the snoring. Sometimes, the Russian just did not seem to care about his job.

I asked his fellow crew members what it was like to work with him. They said he was a great guy. When I asked how he was as a painter, they just repeated that he was a great guy. Later, I found out that the Russian, like most the other privileged Boneyard painters, had worked with Rocky on the North End paint crew about a decade earlier. Ah, now we were getting some place!

One of the few rules the Paint Department enforced was that no matter what we did during the workday, we were absolutely *not* supposed to be in the painters' locker room before 3:10. Despite this rule, once a week for years, we would enter the locker room at 3:10 to find the Russian, playing solitaire in a fancy polo shirt and shorts, already showered and clean-shaven, ready to head to his other job as a tennis instructor. It was hard not to laugh at this man who was so openly indifferent to Department rules, but if Rocky did not care that he didn't care, then I certainly didn't concern myself with it, either.

One afternoon near quitting time, most of the painters were waiting in the break room to sign out. When I walked in, I noticed that everyone was quieter than usual, and then my eyes fell on the Russian playing cards with two women. This was fairly remarkable since there was rarely anyone but painters in our break room, let alone two well-dressed, pretty women. When the Russian realized we were wondering in amazement what was going on, he excused his rudeness, introduced his guests in broken English, and told us he was going to be taking them on a tower tour. One girl was a former Russian actress, and the other was the wife of a Russian politician. They spoke no English but were very polite and took the time to meet each of us with a smile and a handshake, which was more than their chaperone had done with me in five years!

All the way home that afternoon, I was thinking to myself, "Wow, this Russian is a very intriguing guy... but will someone please tell me if he can paint?"

Like the other crews, the Boneyard crew also had three painters' shacks on the West Sidewalk. I do not recall ever seeing any painters in them, though. This was probably because the crew rarely worked on the Bridge and had their own well-equipped crew tent in the Boneyard. I think they only used their shacks when a painter was sick or hung over. They were not heartbroken when their paint shacks were taken from the Bridge and were unmoved by our loss. Their short-sightedness would come back to haunt them a couple of years later.

The Golden Gate Bridge is a national landmark and thus deemed a terrorist target. With the emergence of new Homeland Security measures after the 9/11 terrorist attacks came the installation of many security cameras in secret spots on and around the Bridge. These cameras were meant to deter terrorist activity on the Bridge, but it did not take a genius to quickly realize that they would also be a covert means for management to monitor its employees. This should have been a less-than-subtle indication that even our more discreet Paint Department perks might be in jeopardy.

One morning during work hours, some of the Boneyard crew painters were caught on camera exiting a back gate of the Boneyard, heading to their cars, and driving away. Boneyard painters had been doing this for years undetected, but a newly installed camera had caught them in the act. I guess the evidence must have been overwhelming because Rocky conceded to management's punishment demands without a fight. Within days, the huge Boneyard crew tent was dismantled and leveled. The same maintenance superintendent and ironworkers who took our shacks away oversaw the razing of the tent.

The Boneyard crew stayed afloat but with much less freedom. A few years later, Barney, Roger, and the Russian retired, and the Boneyard crew was permanently dissolved. By the time I retired, the Boneyard served as a storage area for all departments on the Bridge. All that remained of the Paint Department down there was a seldom-used sandblast booth and a hazardous waste station.

Complacency and a lack of accountability brought an end to the Boneyard crew's tenure, just as they had to our shacks and condos a couple of years earlier. Another long-lived Golden Gate paint tradition had been exterminated, one whose likes will never be seen again on the Bridge again.

CHAPTER 8

SOUTH TOWER LEGS

The South Tower legs are a formidable structure.

A VIEW THROUGH THE FOG

The first few years I worked at the Bridge, my crew split time between our sandblast projects and painting jobs we had at the South Tower Pier. At that time, we were the only sandblast crew, and our biggest priority was blasting and re-coating floor beams located under the road deck. These floor beams would be chosen from the Bridge inspectors' "worst of" list. Prior to our starting, ironworkers would go in and build a contained sandblast worksite on one of the scaffolds under roadway. The ironworkers took about six weeks to build the containment, and while we waited, we would attend to our secondary job at the bottom of the tower legs on the South Tower Pier.

Our project at the South Tower Pier involved work on the drainage system that ran across the cell floors at the bottom of each tower leg. The drains had become clogged, and it was our crew's responsibility to assess the problem and fix it. This network of drains was located throughout the tower floors and connected through a grid of small cells. Each cell had steel walls, and most were no larger than 6' × 6', and about 12' in height. There were dozens of these dark little rooms at the bottom of each tower leg. You could reach them by climbing down stationary ladders through hatches and traversing side portholes with only a small light on your hard hat. It was very easy to get lost in this maze of dark enclosures.

The floors of the cells had narrow drains running through them, each channel about an inch wide and an inch deep. They appeared to be only small cracks running from one wall straight into another, and in some cells, intersecting drains would run to and from all four walls. Actually, each was only a small part of a vast network of drains that were all connected, and when working efficiently, were an ingenious method of draining moisture out of the tower legs and keeping water from settling anywhere within the base of the tower. Displaced standing water in any area of the Bridge could cause all sorts of structural problems if not handled properly. To prevent this, the original engineers of the Bridge constructed the tower bases to stand a fraction of an inch higher at one end, creating a slight angle and enabling the drain system to run freely through the cells, and out the lower end.

Rust had started to infect the drains in many of these cells. It was our job to clear the drains out, especially where the small openings at the bottom of the walls had rusted shut. Each one had to be cleared, because if any remained blocked, it stopped the flow of the entire system. Our Foreman had a site map of the entire drainage system, and we were to clear out each cell's drain, one at a time, so that eventually the big picture of complete drainage would come together.

Only one painter could fit in a cell at a time, so we each took our own cell to work in. We first had to chisel and needle-gun the rust out of these little steel channels that ran through the concrete floors, then prime coat them with zinc and finish them with a coat of tar.

Cluttered work sites became a huge problem as we dragged in the necessary equipment. We used droplights in the pitch-black darkness. We needed breathing lines for our air-fed hoods, which we were required to wear in those confined spaces. The tools we used were pneumatic, meaning they ran on air pressure, which required additional air lines. With six painters working simultaneously in six different rooms and all the air lines needed for each operation, our work area would at times look like a big bowl of spaghetti.

Immediately after starting our drain project, we discovered another problem which needed to be addressed before we could proceed. An angled extension went completely around each tower leg. Each extension protruded about three feet and stood about 25 feet up the leg from the base. There was a major rust problem where the extension abutted the tower leg. Huge rust holes had developed, and moisture was running down the towers straight through these holes and into the cells. Therefore, if we wanted to stop the rusting in the drains, we had to first repair the problems created by the rusting on the exterior walls.

As unusual as this may sound, Golden Gate Bridge painters rarely paint the tower exteriors. It is not their priority. The federal funding received is based solely on maintaining the structural integrity of the Bridge, not cosmetic painting. Since the tower is only an aesthetic shell surrounding the true inner structure, exterior tower painting was considered cosmetic. The official responsibility of the Paint Department is maintenance painting, not that we never paint the tower exteriors, but we usually have plenty of preventive maintenance painting to keep us busy.

In this case, we got approval to paint the base of the tower because the repair work would be essential to keeping water out of the cells. Ironworkers hung wires from the underside of the roadway, over 200 feet above, for the swing stages we would work from to paint the 25-foot-high tower bases. We felt it would have been an ideal opportunity to completely paint the 200-foot-tall lower tower exteriors while the stages were hung, but management wanted us to focus only on painting the bases, so the towers would just have to wait patiently for their turn to be beautiful again.

The tower leg base and cell drain repair projects kept our crew working on the South Tower Pier for the next four years. Thus, we became known as the South Tower Crew.

Tourists often asked how we navigated up and down the towers. They wanted to know if there was a big ladder inside the tower that we climbed or whether the only way to the top of the towers was to walk the main cable up. "Yes" and "yes" might have been our answers on some occasions, and this always got a few "oohs" and "ahhs," enhancing the mystique of our job in their eyes. The truth is far less exciting.

There is an elevator inside each tower's East Side. You enter the elevator at roadway and can take it 500 feet up or 200 feet down. It is an old Otis elevator, installed in 1936, and it looks more like a freight elevator than a personnel carrier. The compartment is very confined, with a maximum capacity of three riders, and no matter how small in stature the riders might be, it makes for a cramped ride. You enter through a thin sliding metal-screen gate, and you exit from an identical metal gate on the other side of the compartment when you get to your destination. The elevator runs on an electric cable system and can only be operated when all doors and latches are shut, not only in the elevator, but throughout the entire shaft.

The first two riders get on the elevator one by one, and each one squeezes into a back corner, facing the wall. The painter who will operate the elevator on this trip then steps in, turns to face the metal-screen door, and pulls it shut. Now all three riders are crammed in with their backs to each other, and trust me, when three big guys are in the elevator together, it can be one extremely tight ride. The operator then maneuvers the up/down lever and guides the elevator into just the right spot, lined up with the porthole hatch door at the destination stop. These oval hatch doors are barely large enough to duck through, and if things are not properly lined up, can be difficult to enter. One rider pulls back the elevator's screen door opposite the one they entered through, and then he and the other rider exit the elevator through the little oval hatch door. The operator must remain to go up and retrieve two more riders.

Obviously, this can be a time-consuming process, especially when more than one crew needs elevator access. Each ride to the pier can take five minutes down and five minutes back up. It would require as much as 30 minutes to make the three rides necessary to get our crew of six painters plus a paint laborer to the pier. Naturally, some of the less ambitious workers on our crew could get a half-hour reprieve every day just by making sure they were the last ones down the elevator.

There were strict district rules concerning elevator use, and we were reminded of these regularly by management. But once the South Tower door was shut, elevator anarchy became our way, and rules ceased to exist as long as no one got hurt or damaged the elevator.

Each of the eight elevator stops in the tower has a buzzer, and when pushed, it lets the operator know that somebody on another level needs the elevator. The elevator and its cables are very sensitive to any movement. From any stop, you can look into the elevator shaft and know if it is in operation by the movements of the cables going up or down. Ripples in the cables usually tell you that an elevator is being loaded or unloaded. The sound of the metal doors shutting will usually indicate to a good ear how far away the elevator is and can echo over 500 feet through the shaft.

Any sudden movements inside the elevator cause a lot of noise throughout the shaft. One painter was a one-man wrecking crew and an elevator menace. New painters and others who happened to step into the elevator with this man alone could be in for a wild elevator ride, sometimes highlighted by a good-natured (fully clothed) "man hump."

If we heard the elevator shaking violently, we assumed this guy had discovered it was some painter's birthday, and he had the painter trapped in a corner giving him a "birthday ride." If he asked when your birthday was, it was best to keep quiet. For this reason, I kept my birthday a secret for years.

Sometimes we didn't want to take quite so long getting to our work site. For these times, we had a way of adding two more riders. Having more than three passengers at one time and riding on top of the elevator were items number one and two on management's "Do Not Do" list and grounds for being fired. *Our* only rule, however, was "rules were made to be broken."

To take on more riders, the operator would get in the elevator alone and lower it about eight feet until the roof was at floor level. Two riders would climb onto the roof and grip the cable that held up the elevator. There was very little room on top, so both riders would stand face to face, leaning in, both hanging onto the same cable (close proximity here demanded fresh breath!). The operator would then bring the elevator back up to its original position and pick up two more riders. This way, five riders could ride at once, leaving off four instead of two at each destination.

When they reached their exit point, one rider on top would flip the latch on the door, immediately stopping the elevator, and the two on top would continue up and let out two more riders from the inside. Later, when we spent a lot more time up in the struts, this method of crew transport became the norm.

The first couple of times riding on top of the elevator could make you nervous, especially when you realized you were traveling through a dark shaft hundreds of feet up on top of a little metal box and could fall off to one side or the other and not hit anything on your way down until you reached the bottom. A sure death. To top this off, there might have been some wise guy inside the elevator who thought it was funny to shake it hard and scare the heck out of you. After a few rides, you got used to it and saw that you would have to be a complete fool to fall off—but that did not necessarily exclude any of us.

One morning I was that complacent fool and almost paid the price. Our crew was heading down to the pier to work. There were three painters inside the elevator, and I was alone on the top. I was wearing a down jacket that morning, and as we descended, the bottom of my jacket hooked onto one of the door latches we passed. The jacket was thick, and I did not realize what had happened until the entire back of it was up over my head. Next thing I knew, I was hanging by my jacket as the elevator continued downward.

I yelled, "Stop! Hey, stop!" but since I was in a panic with my jacket over my face, the words must have been muffled because the elevator did not stop.

Finally, I screamed, "Stop the elevator!" and luckily someone heard this time. The elevator came to a stop about ten feet below me. "Come back up. I'm stuck!" I pleaded.

Smokey opened the flop door on top of the elevator and peering up must have been elated to see my predicament. With a dumb-founded look, he asked, "What the hell are you doing up there?"

With hindsight, there are so many things I now wish I had said in response to that, such as, "Oh, nothing, just hanging around, you idiot." However, all my humbled state would allow me to do was beg him to come get me. I'm sure I looked silly dangling there with my coat up over my head screaming for help, but I certainly didn't care at that moment. I knew how lucky I was that Smokey heard my scream and that the elevator did not just keep going, leaving me hanging hundreds of feet above.

CHAPTER 9

ONE SIZE FITS ALL

The east sidewalk can be an active splendor on a nice sunny day.

A VIEW THROUGH THE FOG

In 1915, Edward Dickinson Bullard set out to design a helmet to protect miners from head injury caused by falling objects. His design was based on a World War I helmet worn by soldiers called the "doughboy." The "Hard Boiled Hat," so called because of the steam used in the manufacturing process, was patented in 1919.

Joseph Strauss strove to maintain the safest work environment possible while building his great bridge. One problem the Bridge project faced was serious injuries because of falling rivets. To address this, Edward Bullard created a durable industrial hard hat modeled from his mining helmet. Strauss set up America's first designated "Hard Hat Area" at the Golden Gate Bridge construction site in 1933. Hard hats have always been essential to the work done at the Golden Gate Bridge, and nearly 90 years later, the Bullard Hard Hat Company is still the Bridge's exclusive hard hat supplier.

Hard hats protect your head against many dangers, most notably against falling debris. They are required to be always worn by employees on the Bridge. Personally, I can attest that a hard hat saved me from potentially serious head injury more than once.

A Bullard spokesperson visited our crew room one day with a sample of a new hard hat for us to try. He mentioned that all the new style of hard hats were one size fits all and then rattled off a bunch of technical data: more protection… saves lives… blah, blah, blah. Finally, he got to the topic I cared about: this new style had a knob on the back to adjust the size of the band that keeps the hat in place. This made it easy to tighten or loosen so you could quickly get it on or off your head. I was delighted.

At that time, we had a painter on the Bridge who had a big head. No, really, Greg had a big head! I know little about head measurements, and I've been told that I have a fat head myself, but this guy's head was huge. Greg was tall, which made his head somewhat proportional to his body, but painters still loved to joke with him about it.

Sometimes, we would call him "The Great Gazoo." Now, for those of you who do not know, Gazoo was a character on *The Flintstones*. He was a little floating alien who wore an enormous space helmet, making his head look twice the size of his body. Heinz rode his motorcycle to work, and his helmet was huge. When he passed by our commuter van each day on his bike, someone would always shout, "Hey, there goes Gazoo!"

After the Bullard sales agent was gone, we were all fussing over the sample hard hat he had left. Greg came in, and somebody said, "Look, dude, a hard hat that will actually fit your head."

Greg examined the hat, then turned the knob until it extended the head band as far as it could go, looking large enough to fit a watermelon. Calmly, he replied, "No, it won't."

"The hard hat guy said it's one size fits all, and that would mean even your fat head," said the painter.

Greg placed the fully opened hat on his head, and I could not believe my eyes. It didn't fit! With no change to his expression, he said, "See, I told you."

Someone shouted, "Oh, my God, you are a freak!" We all laughed, and even Greg couldn't help but smile.

He went into Rocky's office with the hat resting just above the top of his head. "Rocky, I need a bigger hat."

Rocky, never looking up from what he was doing, murmured, "One size fits all." When he finally turned his attention to Greg, he smiled, shook his head, and said, "Geez, Greg. Okay, I'll call Safety and see what they suggest."

I did not give the incident much thought after that. I guess Heinz just kept wearing his old hard hat. Then, about a month or so later, we were having our monthly Paint Department safety meeting in the boardroom. All painters were in attendance, as well as our Safety Director and the Bridge Manager, Kary Witt. Mr. Witt had a distinguished older gentleman with him. He introduced his guest as the grandson of Edward Bullard, founder of the Bullard Hard Hat Company. Mr. Witt gave a brief presentation on Bullard Hard Hats and the company's long relationship with the Golden Gate Bridge.

It was an impressive introduction, and I remember us clapping as Mr. Bullard approached the podium. Smiling graciously, he spoke. "Thank you, thank you. Bullard is what it is because of the Golden Gate Bridge. That will always be true, but I'm not here to talk about our company. I actually flew here to see for myself this man who actually couldn't fit into our "one size fits all" hard hats."

We all looked around at each other, laughed, and pointed to Greg.

Then Mr. Bullard looked at Greg, and the expression he made was one I will never forget. His eyes bulged as a look of fascination came over his face. He said only one word: "Oh."

Mr. Bullard kept his eyes focused on Greg and walked around the big table to where he sat. He stood over Greg, fumbled in his pocket, then pulled out a tailor's measuring tape. This man was prepared! Holding the tape out, he asked, "May I?"

Greg grinned, "Sure!"

Mr. Bullard carefully wrapped the tape around Greg's head. The room was completely silent. We were all on the edge of our seats. This was by far the most interesting safety meeting we'd had in a long time. Mr. Bullard finished his measuring, rested his hand on Greg's shoulder, and with a big smile said, "Son, that is amazing. I am going to have a hard hat made especially for you."

Greg beamed, and we all cheered.

CHAPTER 10

JUMPERS THROUGHOUT THE YEARS

The east sidewalk can be a lonely place on a gloomy, overcast day.

A VIEW THROUGH THE FOG

As of 2019, an estimated 1,700 people had jumped from the Golden Gate Bridge, with only 25 known survivors. The number of deaths will be considerably higher if including those who jumped at night, whose suicides went unrecorded. During the last few decades, an average of nearly 30 people a year have jumped off the Bridge.

Profiles of jumpers were not kept during the Bridge's early years, but with the information we have from past jumps and the accurate records kept now, we know some trends and some characteristics of the jumpers. Jumpers are almost exclusively from the Bay Area, with the average age being 41. Jumpers' occupations have varied over the years. Professors and students usually lead the list, with suicide jumps by software engineers recently on the rise. About 80% of the jumpers are white, and 56% are single.

The East Sidewalk is the setting for almost every jump. The sidewalk is a ten-foot-wide concrete walkway that runs the length of the Bridge, taking gradual turns around each tower. A safety barrier, constructed in 2002, protects pedestrians from the roadway, separating the sidewalk from Lane One. Metal latched emergency gates were installed about every hundred yards for Bridge Patrol and tow service to access the sidewalk from the roadway.

The sidewalk's outer steel guardrail is slightly over four feet tall and runs the length of the Bridge. Supposedly, we can attribute the low rail height to Bridge designer Joseph Strauss having been only five feet tall. Beyond the outer rail, three feet below the outside edge of the sidewalk, is a three-foot wide steel box chord, which is the only thing between the outer rail and the 240-foot fall to the waters below. Because of the constant fog and moisture in the air, the top of the chord is wet nearly all the time and can be extremely slick—very dangerous conditions for those of us accustomed to walking on steel every day, let alone a nervous person climbing down onto it for the first time.

A victim caught on surveillance video learned a tragic lesson about the dangers of going over the outer rail. The late-evening footage shows a middle-aged man standing alone on the sidewalk near a light pole, not another soul in sight. Fog blankets the Bridge on this dark, drizzly night. The heavy mist gives the sidewalk lighting an eerie, faded glow, just enough to help guide him over the guardrail. Awkwardly, he climbs over the rail and now stands on the chord ready to jump.

Suddenly, he appears to be having second thoughts about his decision. He does not want to jump. He seems scared and disoriented. Not ready to end his life, he takes a deep breath and gets up his nerve to climb back over the rail to safety.

Reaching for the handrail, he comes up considerably short. Due to the drop from the sidewalk to the chord, the top handrail is now over seven feet above him. The chord glistens with moisture and must be very slick. The man can only reach the bottom of the guardrail, which he now tightly holds onto, searching for a foothold that will allow him to hoist himself back over the rail. His foot slips from the beam, and his grip fails him. He falls back down to the wet chord and slips off, out of sight of the video camera and ultimately gone forever, falling to his death. He learned the hard way how slick and dangerous the outer chord can be and will never get his second chance at life.

Harold B. Wobber, a 47-year-old World War I veteran, walked the pedestrian sidewalk in August 1937, just a few months after the Bridge was opened. Another man strolled alongside him when Wobber suddenly took off his coat, threw it to his companion, and said, "This is where I get off. I'm going to jump." The other man grabbed Wobber, but Wobber broke free and threw himself over the rail. Wobber officially became the first person to jump off the Golden Gate Bridge.

Since Wobber's jump over 80 years ago, Bridge jumpers have chosen many different ways to end their lives. Some park their cars in the lots at either end of the Bridge and walk to the spot they choose to jump from. There are also impulse suicides, involving those who just stop their car, run to the rail, and go up and over. Still others go down onto the outer chord below the guardrail and just stand there, contemplating the reasons that brought them to this point, taking in the last few breaths they will ever take before leaping.

Many jumpers have left suicide notes. Apologies, health issues, and, of course, references to sour relationships head the list of fateful subjects. Sometimes, the notes can be heart-wrenching, like the tragic note left by a young pre-med student from UCLA in 1954, who followed his father off the Bridge just four days after his father had committed suicide. The note read, "I am sorry... I want to keep Dad company."

Kyle Gamboa, a high school student from Fair Oaks, near Sacramento, skipped school one day in September 2013 to jump off the Bridge. *The New York Times* reported he had repeatedly watched the trailer for Eric Steel's documentary, *The Bridge* (mentioned later in this chapter). He yelled, "Yahoo!" as he leaped to his death. His suicide note read, "I'm happy. I thought this was a good place to end."

For decades, disturbing tales and accounts have circulated around the Bridge about those who desired more than just an end to their lives and wanted to make a statement as well. Occasionally, a selfish man, not wanting to leave anything behind, will jump with his life savings in his pocket. There are those who committed criminal acts, taking computers or other incriminating evidence over the side with them. In one case, a 70-year-old man jumped after murdering his wife.

One tragic account involved a couple making a lovers' leap together. Some sort of pact, over the rail hand in hand, four last seconds together. Jumpers have taken their pets with them. Most of the time they hold on to their pets when they jump, but I remember one sad instance when I watched a man toss a helpless dog over before jumping himself.

Pets are not the only ones who go over the rail unexpectedly. Terrible incidents have taken place where jumpers, in their moment of spontaneous desperation, take innocent people over the rail with them. One man got into an argument with his girlfriend near the South Tower. He became so upset that he forcefully shoved the woman up and over the guardrail and then followed her over the side. Both died, but the girlfriend unfortunately did not get to choose where she landed and missed the water, hitting the concrete fender that surrounds the pier.

On January 28, 1993, Steven Page killed his wife Nancy in their Fremont house with a 12-gauge shotgun. Page then drove his 3-year-old daughter Kellie to the Golden Gate Bridge. Highway patrolmen approached Page who looked suspicious as he carried his child across the Bridge sidewalk, causing him to immediately throw his daughter over the rail and then jump himself. A note Page had left earlier, telling how sorry he was about the murders he would commit, confirmed that the terrible incident had been premeditated.

Until the shocking Kellie Page murder in 1993, the youngest death had been 5-year-old Marilyn Demont in 1945. With the child standing on the chord just outside the Bridge railing, her father, August Demont, a 37-year-old elevator installer, commanded her to jump. After Marilyn jumped, her father followed her over. A chilling note later found in his car read, "I and my daughter have committed suicide."

Fellow painters told me of an incident they'd witnessed a couple of years before I came to the work at the Bridge. A man stood next to a random young girl he did not know. He suddenly grabbed the girl, intending to jump off the Bridge with her in his arms. Luckily, several people in the vicinity wrestled the girl from his grip, saving her from a horrific fate. The man jumped alone.

It is hard to grasp the state of mind of someone whose own demise is not enough so that in a moment of senseless desperation they choose to add the murder of an innocent victim to their final act.

Eric Steel's documentary film, *The Bridge*, came out in 2006. The project focused on suspicious people who might consider jumping off the Bridge and attempted to record their jumps on film. Steel and his crew set up stationary surveillance cameras in various locations, filming the Golden Gate Bridge day and night. Telephoto and wide-angle cameras captured 10,000 hours of footage, recording 23 suicides on the Bridge in 2004.

The project became a viral sensation for a while. Consequently, there was an actual spike in suicide attempts after the release of the documentary. Legal issues prompted removal of the film from the Internet shortly after its release. Bridge officials called the film an "invasion of privacy." Also, Steel's permit was an obvious deception, stating his intentions as wanting to "capture the powerful, spectacular intersection of monument and nature that takes place every day at the Golden Gate Bridge."

The film received mixed reviews. Some critics called it nothing more than morbid and unethical voyeurism. *The New York Times* called it "gripping viewing, but you feel like a voyeur of somebody else's pain." Andrew Pulver of *The Guardian* said that it "could be the most morally loathsome film ever made."

Steel defended his film as an anti-suicide project. He stated that most of the film focused on heartfelt interviews with loved ones the suicide jumpers had left behind. Steel argued that he may have prevented at least six suicides when his film crew pointed out suspicious characters to Bridge security officers, who removed the potential jumpers from the Bridge. He also has on film a woman's life being saved when a passerby pulled her back over the rail.

Of course, this is not where the controversy lies. We are a voyeuristic society by nature. We desire to be indulged and shocked by reality TV and "fake news." The public interest and curiosity in Steel's film could not only be attributed to the lives that were saved but also to those that were lost.

Of the 23 suicide jumps that occurred in 2004, there is one I remember all too well. I experienced the Sprague jump live from a different angle and had a much different perspective than I did when I saw it on Steel's video. You *see* a suicide jump on film; you *feel* a suicide jump in person. You know he may jump, but when he does, you are still shocked. And this is followed shortly by the overwhelming grief of seeing the lifeless body afloat on the bay. A fellow human being was just alive, but now he's dead. Steel successfully recorded the acts but failed to capture the essence of the lost souls who provided his footage.

CHAPTER 11

TOWER SHOWER

A great view of the South Tower Pier from above—our own little concrete island on the bay.

A VIEW THROUGH THE FOG

One of the most unusual occurrences I have ever witnessed took place at the South Tower Pier. Those of us involved can never explain all the details of the act without listeners thinking us mad.

The entrance to the South East Tower elevator was the setting, and the members of my paint crew were the players. Now, before I introduce the star, allow me to describe the scene. Coming from the South Tower pier, you climb an 8-foot ladder onto a steel-grated platform which leads you into the tower through one of the oval security doors. Inside, there is a narrow cell leading to the elevator, which you can walk right into when the elevator is at the bottom.

Our crew used the aforementioned method of sneaking extra riders onto the roof of the elevator, but since the elevator stopped at the very bottom and could not go below our entry point, the two roof riders had to climb a 15-foot ladder and wait at the next elevator stop. When the elevator got up to this spot, the operator popped the door and lowered the elevator. Then the two painters stepped onto the roof, shutting the door behind them and all five riders continue up to the roadway.

This particular time, our paint laborer, Junior, had been up at the roadway and was on his way back down to retrieve us. There were five of us still waiting, so it would take two trips to get us all up. The entire group was in position for him when he reached us. One person would need to ride on top, so Smokey decided to make the 15-foot climb to the top of the cell, where he would wait for the elevator to pick him up.

Stew and Robin would be the first to ride the elevator with Junior. The waiting area was cramped even with only two painters in there, so Kevin and I waited out on the landing until the other painters were loaded onto the elevator and heading up. I remember it was a foggy morning and a mist was blowing across the pier. When the outer door was open, it was not uncommon for the fog to drift into the elevator area.

Junior was still not down with the elevator yet, and the rest of us were casually chatting when I happened to glance through the doorway of the cell where Stew and Robin were waiting. Both were leaning against the steel walls of the cell, looking down at the floor. Then, I saw something that made no sense at all: there was actually more mist permeating the cell than there was outside at that moment.

Something else unusual caught my attention, and all I could say was, "Stew, your hair!" Stew had a short Afro and wore no hard hat at that moment. I could see that his hair was dotted with hundreds of little yellow moisture beads.

Finally realizing what must be going on, I thundered, "Smokey!" He was above, peeing directly into the cell they were standing in. The stream was ricocheting off the wall above them, breaking up into a vile mist, and spraying the entire cell.

Robin yelled, "What the f—!" and both he and Stew scrambled out of the cell as I made room for them to pass. At the same time, Kevin went dashing in, and I said, "Where the hell are you going? Don't go in there!"

But like a mother running into a burning house to save her baby, he bellowed, "My coat is in there!" as he grabbed his urine-drenched jacket and darted back out, swearing.

Stew was freaking out and frantically attempting to dry his hair with old paint rags, his face contorted in distress. Robin stood with pee soaking into his shirt and dripping off his hard hat.

Just then, Junior landed the elevator, opened the metal doors, and not having any idea what had happened, said mildly, "Okay, who's first?"

We all simultaneously put our hands up to stop him from exiting the elevator, shouting "No, no, don't get out!"

When Junior asked what was up, Robin yelled, "That stupid jackass is peeing on us!"

"Huh?" Junior said. "Pissing on you?" He immediately shut the elevator doors and took the elevator back up to where Smokey was.

I heard the elevator door open and Junior say, "What you doin' up here, buddy?"

"Nothing. Why?" Smokey answered in a flustered tone.

"Well, you just peed on everyone's head," came Junior's voice. "Look down."

I guess Smokey was finally realizing what he had done, but if you knew Smokey, you would understand that he had a hard time accepting responsibility, much like an ill-mannered toddler. "Well... I had to pee," I heard him answer defiantly.

Junior responded, "You can't pee on people's heads just because you gotta pee, dummy!"

The rest of the crew was still screaming from beyond the doorway, and I could tell Smokey was getting nervous and maybe even a bit scared now.

"I didn't pee on anyone," he insisted. "I didn't know I was peeing in the cell. I thought I was peeing in the elevator shaft." This could have perhaps been true if he had accidentally turned around 180 degrees.

Junior, now frustrated, responded, "And why would it be okay to pee in the elevator shaft? Hell, I had the elevator down there, and you would have been peeing on me, idiot!"

Smokey didn't answer, but Junior told us later that he was visibly shaking at this point. Junior knew what he had to do. "Smokey, pull your pants up, and get in here! I'm going to take you to the top, and you can go on in because if these guys get a hold of you right now, they are going to kill you. They still may kill you later, anyway." With that, Junior took Smokey back up to the roadway.

Within 30 minutes of our scooter returning to the yard, the entire Paint Department was in an uproar. Many painters were calling for Smokey's head. Most could not believe what had happened. If I had not seen it with my own eyes, I wouldn't have believed it myself. The joking started almost right away, and I must have heard a dozen different "golden shower" jokes by the end of the first afternoon.

Obviously, our Paint Superintendent was disappointed with Smokey not only because of the act itself but also because Rocky knew his own critics were condemning his decision a couple of years earlier to hire this 55-year-old painter with health issues and an attitude. Rocky probably wished he could throw Smokey to the wolves but ultimately showed him mercy; he, at least, heard out his story and took depositions from those of us who were there.

While deliberations took place, they sent Smokey home for three days on paid administrative leave. Over those next few days, we had several crew meetings which, as you can imagine, were quite animated. Smokey's misdeed had made the Paint Department look bad and our crew look inept. We had a choice to make, and our options were clear. It was all one man's doing, so we must choose to either implement damage control and stand behind our comrade or throw him under the bus.

Crew Foreman Tiller was shocked and embarrassed by what had happened but backed Smokey and allowed for the possibility that maybe it really had been an accident.

Stew, the crew's veteran leader, who had known Smokey for 20 years, backed Smokey and Tiller unconditionally. Neither Kevin nor Junior, our crew's two biggest clowns, took a side, welcoming the emergence of a new lightning rod on the crew.

Robin, on the other hand, took great offense at what had happened to him that morning and never let up on Smokey. He took the incident to our painter's union, which immediately backed Robin and argued for Smokey's termination. The more Robin pushed the issue with the union, the more Tiller backed Smokey. The division reached a point where it began affecting our crew's work. Smokey and Robin were required to work on different job sites.

Rocky finally stepped in. To appease the situation, he offered Robin a position on the Boneyard crew, basically throwing Robin a bone, hoping to get him to drop his grievance with the union. It worked. Robin jumped at the Boneyard position.

Backlash was quickly directed at Rocky for this because many long-time painters had waited years for one of the coveted Boneyard spots. Now it was obvious that Rocky had given in to pressure, and his decision suggested that in order to get something good in the Paint Department, you must be involved in something bad.

When Smokey returned from his 3-day leave, Tiller made him spend a whole day scrubbing the cells he'd peed in and pay to have everyone's urine-soaked clothes cleaned.

Smokey and I had a unique relationship, due, I am sure, to the fact that we spent an hour alone together in a paint shack every morning and afternoon. Smokey could be a caring person at times, but remorse and regret were not two of his strong points. He surely would not let me see him express either one.

Smokey refused to apologize to Robin for his actions. He shook Robin's hand once in front of Rocky to save his job but never actually apologized to anyone.

I told him, "All this would probably just go away if you just apologized to Robin." He ignored me, though, so I added, "Nobody on the planet sides with you on this. You peed on his head!"

It was deposition day. I was the last of our crew members to talk with Rocky about the incident before Smokey's turn. Once I'd finished my statement, I left Rocky's office. I met Smokey outside the door, ready to go in. Something about him was different.

He rarely wore glasses, but today he had on a pair of thick prescription lenses. My eyes traveled to a far corner of the break room, where the Russian was playing Solitaire without his glasses, squinting at the cards. The Russian had loaned Smokey his glasses! Figuring out Smokey's scheme, I looked back at him and shook my head. "Oh, my God! Please tell me that is not your defense. You wouldn't dare play the feeble old man card?" I demanded.

"Shut up; how do I look?" he said under his breath.

"Come here, idiot," I said, pulling his glasses down to the end of his nose. "There, now you look pitiful as hell."

He shuffled past me into Rocky's office and, with a feigned broken voice, said, "Hey Rawwwwk, how about those Giants?" as he pulled the door closed behind him.

I looked over at the Russian again and gave a casual wave, "Hey."

"Hey," he said, squinting to see who I was although I doubt that he even cared.

The next day Smokey was off the hook with a 6-month probation. A brand-new porta-potty was installed at the bottom of the South Tower elevator and others set up in a dozen other spots around the Bridge just in case somebody had to go and could not hold it in. The "incontinent old man routine" must have worked great for Smokey.

Also, the Russian had made himself useful once again, Still, I would wonder, "Can somebody please tell me if the man can paint?"

Smokey never lived this pee episode down. His legend on the Bridge will endure forever in so many odd ways.

CHAPTER 12

SOUTH TOWER PIER

The mighty base of the South Tower Pier, with the foghorn ready to roar.

A VIEW THROUGH THE FOG

The rickety South Tower elevator comes to an abrupt halt, and you know you have reached the last stop, the end of the ride. You make your way through a dim, narrow passageway to a sealed hatch door and feel cold air on your face. The icy air you're feeling is blowing through the louvered vents in the door. You cannot see the ocean yet, but you can smell it: a dank taste of salt. On the door is a lever. Flipping it gives you access through the hatch, where you exit onto a small platform attached to a ladder ten feet above the South Tower Pier.

Here, you feel as though you've just entered a whole new world. Unexplained sights, sounds, and smells immediately heighten your senses to levels you had forgotten you possess. A soft drizzle hangs in the air like fine mist. The chill infuses every breath. Flat clouds of vapor take shape around your face when you exhale. You can smell and taste the salty ocean in the air.

The sky is filled with dark, rolling clouds, doing their best to screen away the morning sunlight. You catch sight of the fog bank drifting across the pier, a deep gray mist, so thick you could cut it with a knife. Next to you, the outer walls of the tower legs are wet and shining, drops of moisture clinging to the steel.

Above you is the exceptional sight of the road deck underside, and all around you, the ocean swells up and is sucked back down again. Below you, just above the choppy surface, hover the gulls, giving their shrill welcoming cries before soaring off into the fog. Then the sudden booming roar of the foghorn, just 30 feet away, wakes you from your daydream, reminding you that you are still alive, especially if you have forgotten to put your earplugs in.

Welcome to the South Tower Pier.

The piers, massive concrete bases that support both legs of the tower, are grounded against the seafloor of the San Francisco Bay, and stretch over 40 feet above sea level. Surrounding the base of the South Tower Pier is an oval-shaped concrete breakwater fender that acts as both a wave break and a barrier to keep ships from crashing into the tower. Between the pier and the fender is a moat, filled with free-flowing seawater. The South Tower Pier is located in the middle of the channel and surrounded by water, whereas its counterpart, the North Tower Pier abuts the shore on the north end.

Working on the pier was a one-of-a-kind experience, like being on my own little concrete island in the middle of the bay, and it offered a unique view of San Francisco that most never see, encompassing Alcatraz, the East Bay, Fort Point, and Marin County. There was always activity in the waters surrounding the South Tower Pier, and I had the pleasure of taking in these wonderful sights for years.

I would watch crab boats heading out to sea in the morning with crab nets stacked up high on their decks. Commercial fishing boats returned at midday, surrounded by flocks of scavenging gulls following above with flittering wings and a cacophony of distant cries, randomly diving to feed on the fish and extra bait the fishermen tossed overboard. Chartered party boats filled with seasick amateur anglers headed out for salmon or rockfish.

Huge oil tankers and freightliners passed through the straits, flying many different flags. Cruise liners would glide so close to the pier, you could look up and see their decks filled with happy vacationers waving down at you as they headed out to sea.

The thrill of sailing brought many people and their boats to the bay. Boat races took place all year long in the San Francisco Bay, but during Fleet Week there were aquatic races every day. The South Tower Pier was a great place to watch these races up close. Racers took to the water in watercraft that ranged from rowboats to dinghies to large yachts; you name it, somebody raced it, and we had front-row seats.

The 2013 America's Cup yacht race was held in the San Francisco Bay. What a sight it was to see these amazing boats passing near the South Tower! The boats were more enormous than I'd ever imagined, and to see their tall mainsails at close range was awe-inspiring and watching the talented crews adjust the rigging and sails fascinating. Observing the speed, grace, and power in person gave me a new respect for a sport I had previously known very little about.

During breezy summer afternoons, surfers and windsurfers made their way through the waves under the Bridge. *How can these dedicated thrill seekers stand the frigid waters?* I wondered.

But this was nothing compared to those who would actually swim under the bridge. Members of the Dolphin Club of San Francisco regularly swam all the way from Sausalito to San Francisco. A little rowboat with a rower and an attendant on a bullhorn accompanied each swimmer, shouting encouragement. Many swimmers did not finish, but I had to give them credit for even getting into that chilly ocean water.

A few times a day, the Red and White Fleet charter boats would make their trip from Fisherman's Wharf, carrying tourists on their loop around the South Tower.

As the charter boats got close, I could hear the garbled words of the captain from the ship's intercom telling the tourists to take notice of the Golden Gate Bridge painters. The tourists turned and waved, some even taking a picture.

This always made me feel like an animal displayed on a zoo safari ride. I never quite knew what to do. *Should I do something to entertain them?* As other painters contemplated such acts as pulling down their pants for the boat, I figured it best to take the high road and just wave to them as they went by. I often wondered exactly what the man on the intercom might say to his passengers as they passed. "Look, everyone, catch a glimpse of the Golden Gate Bridge painter in his natural work habitat!"

Activity around the South Tower Pier was always exciting. No matter what, rain or fog, one thing I could count on every day was seeing a little wooden boat, no more than 25 feet in length. "The Popeye Boat," as Mike and I affectionately named it, would make a slow loop under the Bridge, sometimes struggling against the choppy waves. Its cabin looked to be only a wooden box with a window in front, just large enough for the skipper to stand in and steer the boat. A black pipe extending from the top of the cabin, which acted as a smokestack, added to the boat's charm.

Many times, there would only be a couple of passengers aboard, not leaning on a rail or taking photos of the sights, like most tourists we saw on other boats, but lying on the wooden deck behind the cabin, on top of what seemed to be a makeshift bed. They'd be covered with blankets and, usually sipping on glasses of wine. It seemed like a lovely way to view the Bridge, looking straight up at it as the boat cruised underneath and then circled back around. Surely, a romantic experience.

This boat passed near the pier every day during the 12 years I worked on the Bridge. No matter what we were doing, Mike and I would run to the guard rail when it appeared and wave to the skipper and his passengers as the boat putt-putted by. The captain never failed to return our wave, and even though I never met this man, I felt like I knew him. The boat's humble charm and consistency became a comfort to me. I will never forget "The Popeye Boat."

Given that I spent my days on a bridge made of concrete and steel, I was constantly amazed at all the wildlife I saw during my time there. The wide variety of aquatic life I encountered while working at the South Tower Pier was an unexpected treat.

However, most of the birds on or around the South Tower Pier were not of a pleasant sort at all. They ruled the pier and were relentless in their pursuits to soil it. Concrete and steel fell victim to their horrible barrage of droppings, and the smell could be intolerable. Lucky for us, there was a fire hose on the pier, and our laborer spent most of each morning flushing bird poop over the side of the deck and into the moat.

The number-one crappers were the cormorants, who were a menace to every bridge in the bay area and simply known as "s— birds." These seabirds could not walk ten feet or go two minutes without pooping, and then they would jump into the water and crap again the second they landed. They had voracious appetites, and as far as I could tell, all they did was eat and crap.

Their annoying friends, the seagulls, were not much higher on the sanitary ladder. Seagulls were not only poop machines but also flying garbage cans. We could drop nothing on the deck without a seagull sneaking up behind us and trying to eat whatever it was, whether it be an old paintbrush, a dirty rag, or even a smoldering cigarette butt. Oh, and they loved eating Smokey's used earplugs! The gulls were noisy, too, constantly squawking.

Patience wore thin, and a seagull vs. human battle took place one morning. We had recently come across a gull nest on the pier with eggs in it. I mean, I guess you could call it a nest even though it had been made up from strips of tape, two plastic gloves, and a spray hood we'd left out the day before. As Junior was walking across the pier, he slipped on some seagull crap on the deck and fell.

"Ugh!" His cry of disgust rivaled the roar of the traffic above us. His face twisted in anger.

Enraged, he rushed to the nest, grabbed one of the green-spotted eggs the seagull had been guarding, and fired it, hitting the seagull with its own egg. Hard to figure out who won this battle, but as far as dignity goes, the one with the egg on his face was Junior.

The giant pelicans were always interesting to watch. They would float patiently on the waves, then suddenly flap their large wings several times, lifting their enormous mass up and out of the water. Soaring a foot or two above the surface, wings motionless, they would let themselves be lifted by an air current, and scan the bay from above, looking to swoop down on some seafood delights.

My favorite birds on the Bridge, though, were a pair of peregrine falcons who lived under the roadway near the South Tower. From the pier we could watch them hunt above us. We knew some prey was in trouble when we saw a falcon tuck its wings, swooping down over a hundred feet at blazing speeds to attack a pigeon or sparrow in mid-flight. They also hunted above the road deck, sometimes as high as the tops of the towers. At times, we would discover a tiny bird heart and small beak near the towers at the roadway and figure they were all that remained of a peregrine falcon's unfortunate prey because these were the only parts of a bird that were indigestible. The falcons were such skilled hunters, it was a privilege to watch them in action.

Birds were not the only wildlife we would see from the pier. We were always greeted by some of the many sea lions who fished and frolicked around us all day. We would often see them dive and come up with fish in their mouths. Their sharp pointed teeth did not allow them to chew their food, so we would watch them tossing their heads from side to side, thrashing the helpless fish against the surface of the water until the fish finally ripped apart. Feeding frenzy aside, sea lions usually just looked like they were wishing they could play with us. Sometimes, we'd spot them floating only 20 feet away, their heads poked up out of the water to stare at us. They were always friendly and playful, reminding me of pet puppies, and they did even have a distinct bark when craving attention.

During my time at the South Tower Pier, I also became acquainted with the harbor porpoises. The smallest species of porpoise, the harbor porpoise has a dark gray back, its sides and belly pale gray or white. They are beautiful animals up close. I have lived in the Bay Area my whole life and never knew porpoises were native there.

After working on the Bridge for several years, I noticed that they just seemed to appear in the waters near the South Tower Pier. It turns out that they had not been around for 60 years. According to William Keener of Golden Gate Cetacean Research, the leading theory as to why these porpoises returned to the bay had to do with feeding. Low rainfall had expanded saltwater habitats in the bay for schooling fish such as herring.

I had always enjoyed seeing the dolphin shows at aquatic parks, but it was much more satisfying to see these graceful animals in the wild every day. Porpoises were so elegant, and one of the quickest saltwater mammals. They always looked like they were on a mission to get somewhere, keeping a steady rhythm as they would surface, go under, surface, never breaking their pace. They were gregarious creatures, too. Sometimes, we'd spot two smaller-sized porpoises traveling together, seemingly a couple, and other times, a parent and a baby would swim together.

They would come close to the pier as they swam by, and while it was unclear to me whether they ever noticed us, I certainly noticed them with their sleek, shiny bodies, swimming so effortlessly. I will forget none of my close encounters with these gorgeous animals nor all the other fascinating creatures I got to know while working on the South Tower Pier.

Memories of my time there still tingle my senses. I was dwarfed by the man-made structures towering above and surrounded by the natural beauty of wildlife, surf, and fog; my time spent on the Pier was an escape to a serene oasis amidst the turbulent sea that is everyday life.

A VIEW THROUGH THE FOG

CHAPTER 13

UNPREDICTABLE BEHAVIORS

looking down at the moat surrounding the South Tower Pier from the sidewalk at roadway that veers around the tower

A VIEW THROUGH THE FOG

The infamous San Francisco afternoon wind can create chaos for those walking the sidewalk. There is the poor soul whose hat blows off, which is followed by a quarter-mile chase down the sidewalk, each time reaching for the hat as it blows another ten feet away. Finally, he reaches the hat, only to have it rise up and shoot into traffic. Or the tourist who will discreetly toss a half-drunk cup of coffee over the rail and have it swirl back up and drench the person next to them. Many times, I have witnessed men repeatedly pulling down a shirt that keeps billowing up from the wind to expose a portly vacation belly or a girl frantically fighting with the dress that wants to blow up over her head.

The Bridge's unpredictable wind has a mind of its own and is not always kind. Once, I witnessed the wind do the unthinkable. A young lady was fulfilling the last wish of a loved one by throwing ashes from the Bridge. The girl dumped a bag full of ashes over the outer rail, only to have the entire contents of the bag blow back up, covering herself and the dozen onlookers beside her with ash.

Nine million visitors from all over the world walk the Bridge every year. This makes for a lot of interesting people doing a lot of interesting things, and witnessing so many entertaining distractions on the East Sidewalk, made it nearly impossible to spot someone who might be contemplating a jump.

Bridge security had strict rules concerning conduct on the pedestrian sidewalk, but people can be just as unpredictable as the wind. Odd characters have always found ways onto the sidewalk to risk peril for attention. I witnessed a political protest during the running of the Olympic Torch across the Bridge in April 2008, when protesters ascended the South Tower from the sidewalk and unraveled a huge "Free Tibet" banner. I have also seen a man on a 10-foot unicycle, a clown on stilts, and a woman doing backflips from one tower to the other.

I even had a man speed past me on a high wheeler bike from the 1800s, ringing a little bell. The bike had an enormous front wheel, a tiny rear wheel, and a seat above the front wheel that was raised over five feet off the ground. Each turn of the pedals sent the big front wheel around once, so the bike traveled a long distance with a single turn of the wheel. The rider had no means of turning the bike, no control over his speed, and could not stop the bike if he had to. He just buzzed down the sidewalk, loving all the attention he received, not caring that a single mishap or a big gust of wind could topple him over the outer rail to his death.

Luckily, most tourists on the sidewalk are not there for attention and keep a much lower profile. Many are amateur photographers, arranging poses with a backdrop of the bay: maybe a selfie glamour shot, a silly picture, or a photo taken with a Bridge worker. Others pedal their rental bikes up and down the sidewalk, trying to stay upright as they weave their way through the sidewalk traffic. These are examples of busy tourists, obviously not suicide threats.

Some tourists love to take in the whole Bridge experience, stopping every few feet to catch all angles of the inspired view. They may look out over the rail for hours at the beauty the Bridge offers, soaking up as much scenery as they can.

This is where good judgment on our part must come into play. Many jumpers waste no time in jumping, as I mentioned, but there are those who contemplate their intended leap for hours due to fear, doubt, second thoughts, or maybe just because they are reflecting on their last precious moments on Earth.

It's hard to separate these types of "pre-jump" suspects from those just thoroughly enjoying the beautiful view. Politely approaching the person and striking up a casual conversation to evaluate the situation at hand further was always a good way to confront this dilemma. As my next story will show you, even this can make for a difficult call.

One encounter I had with a potential jumper will never leave me. Although it happened over a dozen years ago, I remember it as though it had occurred yesterday.

It was getting near time for our morning break. We had spent the morning working in the cells located at the bottom of the South Tower. After our elevator ride up to roadway level, I exited the tower onto the sidewalk along with two other painters. We headed to our paint scooter, that is parked beside the tower for our ride back to the painters' break room.

This particular morning's weather, foggy and overcast with a howling wind, drew my attention to a young man at the outer rail looking extremely anxious; he was wearing only jeans and a beige short-sleeved t-shirt. The chilly wind, wet sidewalk, and moisture running down every inch of the surrounding steel did not seem to be the environment a somewhat disoriented sleeveless man should hang out in. This alone did not cause me too much concern since tourists are often caught underdressed because they have misjudged the fickle weather that San Francisco can offer up at any time of year.

Still, as far as I could see, the young man looked to be the only person on the entire East Sidewalk. I asked my fellow workers to give me a couple of minutes to talk with the man. As I got closer, I could see that he appeared to be in his early 20s, unkempt, shivering from the cold, and nervous. He walked toward me as I approached him and seemed as though he wanted to engage in conversation.

Observing his soaking wet t-shirt, I offered, "Looks like a real crappy day for sightseeing."

"I'm not sightseeing," he replied. "I'm waiting for my girlfriend to come by on her bike. She works in the city and will come by here any minute."

I looked around, seeing no sign of anybody coming, and doubted the possibility of anyone being out on a bicycle in this type of weather. "Dude, you are gonna freeze," I said. "Why don't you wait for her at the gift center, or the café, or someplace out of this rotten weather?"

He reached into his pocket then and pulled out a diamond ring. "When she comes by, I'm going to get down on one knee, hold this ring up, and propose to her right here at this tower."

I had to admit, that sounded romantic. Giving him a genuine nod of approval, I smiled and said, "That is really cool."

I began reasoning things in my head. Had he already proposed to her somewhere else, and she'd refused, leaving him depressed enough to contemplate a jump? Maybe no girl existed at all, and he was playing me so I would leave him alone? Or perhaps she was real and actually going to come riding up at any moment, and this young man's gesture would prove to be the most romantic moment of both their lives? I did not know what to believe.

What I knew was that if I reported this man to Bridge Security, his appearance and demeanor would definitely prompt them to come out here to question him, and perhaps they would be interrogating him at the moment the girl arrived on her bike, thus turning the romantic moment into an awkward, embarrassing thing for them.

Once again, I scanned the sidewalk just in case she was out there, but still no sign of anyone coming through the gloomy darkness. Closing my eyes, I contemplated my options one last time, then stretched out my hand, grasped his tightly, and gave the man a genuine smile. "Well, good luck. I know she'll say yes."

"Thank you, thank you. I sure hope so," he replied, smiling.

I jumped into the scooter where my co-workers were still waiting, and we headed in for break. Who was I to stand in the way of true love? Our break ended 30 minutes later, and the weather seemed much more pleasant upon our return to the South Tower. The fog that had clung to the Bridge had lifted, dissipating in the morning's warmth. I wondered how Mr. Romantic was doing and actually smiled at the thought of his success. When I made the turn from the plaza onto the sidewalk, however, I saw the Northbound Number One lane blocked off and a Bridge patrol car at the tower.

My hopes that I might have been part of something special were immediately dashed and replaced by a sense of intimate pain. A pit formed in my stomach: some great misfortune was about to happen.

It was obvious that there was a problem at the tower, but the fear of what I would hear kept me from turning on the portable Bridge radio. The Bridge Patrol officer was on the sidewalk directly in front of the South Tower, looking down over the outer rail. After parking the scooter, I looked around but saw no sign of anybody other than the officer. My bad feeling was getting worse. I headed toward the officer.

"Jumper?" I asked somberly.

"Yeah, a driver reported on their cell phone that they saw a man go over the rail about a half hour ago," answered the officer.

My heart sank as I approached the rail and reluctantly guided my glance downward to what I had hoped not to see. There he was, floating face down in the moat, his beige t-shirt clinging to his lifeless body. It was the young man. I closed my eyes and fought back tears.

The officer could see that I was upset. "Did you know this man?" he asked.

"No, I didn't, but I think I was the last one to talk to him," I managed to say. "Was there any report of another person with him before or after the jump?"

"I haven't heard. Why, was there someone else here with him?"

"No, just curious, thanks," I said.

I will never know whether he proposed and she denied him, or if there was ever any girl at all. It does not really matter anyway because the bottom line is that I feel like I let a man die that day. Had I not favored curiosity over prudence, I could have prevented his death by reporting him and having him removed from the Bridge. I made the mistake of ignoring the obvious signs for the sake of my faith that the good in this situation would prevail.

It took me a while to come to grips with what happened that day. I felt angry at myself, frustrated with him, and sad about the entire ordeal. I still think of him sometimes and wonder what I could have done differently. I have stopped condemning myself over the incident, though, and I realize now that I never could have known for sure what went on in the young man's head that day. No matter his reason for jumping, if there could have been any upside to this tragic event, I had given the young man a genuine smile and a warm handshake before he left this world.

I am now retired from the Golden Gate Bridge Paint Department, but people still ask me, "Wow, you worked on the Golden Gate Bridge? Have you ever seen a person jump?"

I tell them, "Yes, and I pray nobody else ever has to see it again!"

CHAPTER 14

STRUT FOUR

Strut Four. Our crew's bad weather hangout was inside the lowest of the South Tower's four horizontal struts, seen here.

A VIEW THROUGH THE FOG

As I look back on my days as a Golden Gate Bridge painter, a place I will fondly remember is the last of our unofficial crew hideaways on the Bridge. We called it "Strut Four," and it was another one of our discreet hangout spots. The strut was an alternative to the painters' shacks, and our crew spent a lot of time there during the first five years I worked on the Bridge. It eventually became a last place of refuge for us when the shacks and condos were taken away. Strut Four was a very unusual place, and it probably could have had its own wing in a Ripley's Believe It Or Not! museum.

The hideaway was located inside one of the South Tower struts. What in the heck is a strut, you ask? The struts are highly visible parts of the Bridge structure, parts you have probably seen many times. They run horizontally from one tower leg to the other and function as the major tower supports whose intended purpose is to resist longitudinal compression. Each tower has four struts above the roadway. This one got its name because it is the fourth elevator stop from the pier. On days when the elevator was inaccessible, you had to climb exactly 120 ladder rungs to reach the strut from the roadway.

On the afternoons we worked at the South Tower Pier, some of the crew would not feel like riding the 5-10 minutes in a scooter around to the West Sidewalk where our painters' shacks were, especially when tourist traffic was heavy on the East Sidewalk. It was easier to just take the elevator up past the roadway to our alternative retreat in Strut Four.

When people hear about the time we spent in the strut, they are fascinated to know that vehicles were passing directly underneath us as they crossed the Bridge, but I have to imagine that if the drivers knew highly paid painters were lounging in the strut above them during work hours, it probably would have made the $8 toll they'd just paid a little harder to swallow.

The same concept holds true for the struts as it does for the tower legs: what you see on the outside is an aesthetically pleasing exterior shell. Inside, a mass of heavy steel converges at many different angles, and I could not even pretend to know the principles of physics or the engineering calculations involved in this creation.

Upon entering Strut Four from the elevator, you entered a large, dimly lit area by way of a steel-grated catwalk that ran the entire length of the strut. The narrow catwalk was about eight feet above the floor of the strut. This steel floor was the only thing between the catwalk and the roadway traffic below, and it was rusted so badly that you could peer down through its rust holes to see the cars rolling by about a hundred feet below.

For a couple of reasons, you would not be wise to leave the catwalk to go to this strut floor area. First, unseen rust pockets could be anywhere and falling through into the Bridge traffic below was not an appealing prospect. Second, I imagined this floor to have been an open toilet for Bridge workers over the last 70 years. Whenever I would accidentally drop a hard hat down into this abyss, I would just get a new one rather than brave the unknown perils of the strut floor. Painters even second-guess retrieving cell phones or wallets dropped onto that floor.

The strut was 35 feet tall inside. About 20 feet above the catwalk was what appeared to be a wooden ceiling, but it was in fact the underside of a work-platform built years before for the intended use of repairing the rusted ceiling of the strut. We called this the "dance floor." It was a continuous platform about eight feet from the top, and it gave us complete access to the ceiling. The job of repairing the ceiling was our official reason for being allowed to hang out in the strut. This work platform had been erected many years before I showed up, and by the time I left years later, I am ashamed to admit, it was never once used for work. It was just an illusion, a false job set up solely as an excuse for painters to be up there.

One afternoon, our crew was lounging in Strut Four when we were warned that several White Hats were coming up for a routine visit with some board members, and we were to assume our positions at the job site immediately. All of us looked at each other, puzzled, as we had never actually discussed a strategy for this situation. We'd assumed our bluff would never be called. We just shrugged our shoulders, went up top, grabbed any tools on hand, and, as this dog-and-pony show came our way, we plugged the tools in and just started chiseling and grinding the steel directly in front of us. The noise became deafening inside the strut. The tour had no desire to be near our work area, so they just covered their ears, turned around, and hurried back into the elevator. Once they were gone, we got the thumbs up from our laborer, unplugged the tools, climbed down, and went back to our lounging in the shack. No panic... intrusion averted. The sad part was, I felt no guilt.

Strut Five, above us, was occupied by another paint crew. I never went into their strut, but I knew that it was not nearly as special as ours. Both struts were immune to surprise visits because both crews' paint laborers took turns on watch, keeping the elevator at their strut. If any surprise guests needed access at the roadway, they would have to buzz for the elevator, and the laborer would pick them up and alert us if the visitors were in fact on their way to one of our struts. If it was necessary to abandon our hideaway, we were ready to leave it and climb down the ladders in the West leg. Sometimes, White Hats visited our struts unexpectedly, and as they were coming up in the elevator, we were furtively evacuating both struts at the same time, down the backside. This involved coordinating 12 painters to quickly climb down two sets of ladders through hundreds of feet of dark cells.

What made our strut unique was the 80-year-old riveters' shack inside it. The little wooden shack sat off to the left side of the catwalk that ran through the strut, painted International Orange to match all the steel structure around it. This shack had initially been used as a tool depot where riveting tools were stored and issued out. I imagine, during the building of the Bridge in the 1930s, that this shack bustled with activity. Despite any historical significance the little building had had in the past, however, painters had long ago commandeered this relic, and it was now just another crew hideaway for us.

The shack was of simple construction, with a sturdy framework and thick plywood walls. The main room was a 5' × 10' space with a pantry in the back corner. The ceiling stood about seven feet tall. A wooden table stretched about six feet along the back wall, a carpeted bench could seat 3-4 painters, and the floor provided enough room for two painters to sit comfortably. A second room, added about five years before I started, was attached to the main room. This room was considerably smaller, but provided ample space for two painters to relax on the carpeted floor.

This crew shack had a special lock system, similar to the ones devised for our roadway shacks, which made it appear to be locked and uninhabited, even when painters were inside. The shack had electricity running to it and contained two droplights, a space heater, and a 3" portable television inside.

Directly across from the shack, on the other side of the catwalk, sat a work bench with some tools and miscellaneous supplies. Beside this bench were the infamous "pee buckets."

Upon entering the Strut Four crew shack for the first time, I could not believe my eyes. A retired painter called Frog had apparently spent a lot of his spare time expressing his artistic side within this shack's interior. I will do my best to describe his "masterpiece," but as with all great artists, his work must be seen to be believed. I had actually heard rumors about this crew shack and Frog's art even before I started working at the Bridge, and I must admit that it definitely lived up to all the hype.

Frog had spent many hours, days, months, and maybe even years cutting pictures out of magazines and adhering them to every available inch of wall and ceiling in the shack. I never could make sense of his arrangements, but Frog must have had some sort of vision to invest that much energy in something so unusual.

Literally thousands of these little cutout pictures papered the shack. At first glance, one might imagine that the pictures came only from girlie magazines, and most actually had. Upon closer examination, this abstract conglomeration included many types of images. For example, one block of cutouts included photos of an elephant, a girl in a bikini, the Taj Mahal, and a birthday cake.

After a while, I didn't even notice the pictures. To me they were just part of the shack, but it was always comical to watch other painters' reactions when they looked upon these collages for the first time. Personally, I was never exactly awestruck by Frog's arrangements and just mentally filed all of it under "another man's art." Not being much of an artist myself, who am I to judge it as inspiring or trashy?

Some Bridge workers, painters included, considered these pictures vulgar and immoral, and when the time had come for the Paint Department's scandalous ways to be exposed and eradicated, it was a great opportunity for those offended by Frog's art to push for their removal.

Our crew foreman claimed that management knew of the pictures and had told him to have them removed immediately. One morning, two of our painters were sent in to strip every surface of its pictures and remove all the boxes of naughty books that Frog had left behind in the shack. Some painters approved of Frog's art, or at least his right to express himself. To them, this was yet another blow to the traditions of the Golden Gate Bridge painter, and some viewed it as no less than an old Puritan book-burning. After two years of looking at those walls, the art-work removal did not really devastate me. Besides, there was one disturbing picture on that always gave me the creeps: a boa constrictor with a baby goat in its belly.

I never could get any authentic eyewitness accounts about another Frog-related myth I had heard, but one bit of leftover evidence may have been a key to balancing truth and fiction. Rumor was that Frog spent so much of his last couple of years on the Bridge wrapped up in his special projects (which, aside from creating his collages, included whittling duck decoys and polishing rivets) that he would hang around the Strut Four shack in little or no clothing at all. This rumor was spread by a painter who swore Frog had once brought the elevator down to pick up a couple of painters dressed only in his robe and slippers. Now, whether this was an accurate or exaggerated account, I cannot say, but I will attest that I always noticed a small track zigzagging across the ceiling. When I asked about it, I was told that it was where Frog had attached a shower curtain (hmm... shower curtain) that he would pull shut and relax behind when he wanted privacy. Myth confirmed?

I did not feel comfortable lounging in the Strut Four shack for a while after being hired not because I didn't enjoy lounging. I love lounging, but it could get claustrophobic being in such close proximity to six other guys.

After weeks of avoiding the strut crew shack, I realized that hanging around outside of the shack was not exactly desirable, either. There was the matter of two big "pee bottles" sitting across from it. These were large drinking water bottles, each with a big red oil funnel fitted on its top, and painters would not be bashful about using these bottles regularly. The fact that they also contained bleach and disinfectant never made them any less repulsive.

As I mentioned earlier, I hated the cramped space in the Strut Four shack, so I roamed the strut seeking alternate areas to relax. One afternoon, I climbed the 20-foot ladder that led to the "dance floor," our wooden work platform. I was sitting in a chair to pass the time when I noticed something in one of the dark corners of the platform. It was a square piece of plywood attached to the floor by a hinge, barely noticeable in the dim light. I approached and saw that it was some sort of trap door. I grabbed a flashlight and poked my head down into it to discover a tiny, abandoned room. It was completely empty and had a plywood floor, plywood ceiling (the deck I was kneeling on), and riveted steel walls. It was about 3' × 7', and about 3' high, not much larger than the inside of a casket...I assume.

Later, I asked Stew if he knew of this room. He said it had been abandoned for years, but that was all he knew about it. The next day, I snuck in a sleeping bag and some bubble wrap for the steel walls and fashioned a pillow out of rags and a plastic bag. I now had my own little alternative to the cramped crew shack.

I hung a droplight and put a battery-operated clock inside. My private space in Strut Four was ready, and it was a good thing because a time would come when Strut Four would be more than just an occasional hideaway for the crew.

I had been at the Bridge for about five years when a big job came up. It was a sandblast job at the North End under the roadway. Our paint crew was chosen for the job, which was scheduled to take at least three years to complete.

It was called the North Approach Viaduct (NAV) project. We would work on a new platform system called Quick Deck, and we were to sandblast all the steel under the roadway, then prime and finish coat it. The steel had actually been sandblasted 20 years earlier and primed with zinc primer but never finish coated. The primer was now failing, and our job was to re-blast the steel. We had been the only sandblasting crew on the Bridge for years, so we were a natural choice for the project.

One hundred percent containment was to be enforced on this job, meaning we were required to recover all the water we used for washing and all the spent sand from the blasting; there could be absolutely no paint overspray. Quite a challenge lay ahead! Large, shrink-wrapped, vinyl partitions would need to be built to contain the sand. A ventilation system would have to be installed permitting both negative and positive air flow to counter the pressure built up from the sandblasting. Also, a high-powered, high-volume vacuum system had to be implemented to remove the sand as quickly as possible before the weight of it could collapse the deck.

On the ground below, large-capacity blast pots would be needed to handle the four blast hoses we'd be operating at all times, large enough to hold a day's worth of sand, which would amount to at least 4000 pounds. Also, two huge compressors were required to run the blast pots.

Since this was a lead-compliance job, we would also need a Decontamination (Decon) trailer with a shower and clean changing areas, not to mention trailers for each crew to take breaks in. A tremendous undertaking, every aspect of this job would require extensive planning before we could get started.

First, Bridge Maintenance had to level off a work site at the North End to store all our equipment, trailers, and Decon units. Ironworkers would install the Quick Deck and then build our containment areas. Operating engineers would get our blast pots and vacuum in place. Management wanted these other Bridge tradespeople to work on their projects without us being in the way, so we agreed that until the job was ready for us, our crew should stay busy with other paint projects.

Our repair project at the bottom of the tower legs and the cell drains at the pier had been completed, and because of the high-priority sandblast job on the North End, our previous sandblast job under the Bridge deck was put on hold. Consequently, we found ourselves without a job until the NAV project was ready for us. The crew foreman suggested that we temporarily resume our Strut Four ceiling project. The paint superintendent probably didn't even remember that the job existed, but to avoid having to search out new work for us, he agreed to this suggestion.

For a couple of weeks, our crew would go to the North End to watch our future job site develop. Once we realized we were just bringing attention to the fact that we were not busy, however, we gradually implemented a routine that would get us into the tower first thing every morning.

The first couple of weeks, each morning we would drive our scooter past Crew Foreman Tiller, who would give us an emphatic two thumbs up and a big smile, meaning that we should head up to the strut until further notice. After a month of this, our daily strut approval came with one thumb up. After two months, it was a mere salute that directed us to the strut, and by the time three months of this routine were behind us, we just barreled past Tiller in our scooter, not even waiting for his okay. Our crew of six painters and one laborer had reached a point where we expected to go to the Strut Four shack every day.

Each morning, we got to the tower at 7:15 a.m. and left at 2:45 p.m., spending the entire day there except for when we came down for break and lunch. Some days, we would not even leave for these. This was our daily routine for six months.

This backwards way to make a paycheck made for one of the oddest six months of my life. I became attached to my time in Strut Four, as did the rest of the crew. I spent about half of my day relaxing in the private room I had built in the strut. Phone or internet couldn't be accessed from this room, so I usually just passed the time reading books or newspapers. The other half of the time, I stayed in the crew shack with the rest of the guys. The shack had been stripped of its character years before, but it was still a cozy space with a bench, table, and resting spots. Seven painters could squeeze into these two rooms.

There was always food in the shack. Maybe there were a dozen donuts in the morning for us to eat while watching the news on our 3" TV. Somebody might bring in a couple of pizzas after lunch, and there was a Coleman stove where we could cook Jiffy Pop popcorn when it was time for a movie.

We chipped in and bought an 8" DVD player for the shack, but it was never easy to find a movie that seven painters with low attention spans could agree on. Guys would fight for the best spots on the bench to watch the movies and then would usually get bored within ten minutes and just fall asleep. For the next couple of hours, a loud movie with nobody watching it would echo through the strut. Thank goodness for my own little hideaway and my ear plugs!

Our crew became so used to spending every day in the strut that it no longer felt like the privilege it had once been but rather an expected routine. Every couple of weeks, a minor job would come up somewhere else on the Bridge. A pair of us would be expected to handle it, but whenever the time came, we would actually have the gall to complain and wonder why it was our turn and not somebody else's. We all moaned about working two hours a month but couldn't see how ridiculous our complaints were.

I had become complacent and lazy although I didn't yet recognize the change in myself. Despite one's diligence and intent to be an outstanding employee, it is virtually impossible to resist a job perk like this or to even acknowledge the beauty of its existence. Guilt takes on a new meaning. The guilt that lingered in me morphed into doubt, and I wondered whether I'd ever be able to function at a high level in the workplace again.

CHAPTER 15

STRUT FOUR REVISITED

Construction on the long-awaited Suicide Safety Net is an extensive project and has become a necessary priority for the bridge as it nears completion.

A VIEW THROUGH THE FOG

I remember the last time I was in Strut Four. Our six-month stint in the strut eventually ended, and our sandblast job on the North End had begun. Our crew had not visited the strut for over a year, and a lot had changed. The Strut Four shack had been discovered and exposed, and although it still remained, the shack had been stripped of everything but its bench and was now just a supply shed.

On this particular day, inspections being made throughout the Bridge by White Hats. All paint jobs on the Bridge were temporarily halted, and Tiller told us simply to get lost for the whole day. He added that there might be some inspections in the struts, so we should stay out of the Towers, especially the elevators which were going to be used by the White Hats. It was payday Friday, which meant that there was no morning break, so we needed to stay out of sight from 7:00 a.m. until lunchtime. We'd heard on good authority that the White Hats would not be doing any inspecting above the roadway until after lunch. With that in mind, Mike, Smokey, and I took a chance and headed up to our old stomping grounds at Strut Four. To play it safe and avoid the elevator, we climbed the 120 ladder rungs that went up the West Side. We figured that we would just hang out in the crew shack like old times until lunch and then climb back down. What could possibly go wrong?

We found the Strut Four shack filled with work buckets. We cleared them out, stacked them behind the shack, swept the floor, and even found our 3" portable TV hidden in a bag in the pantry. After we watched the news for about an hour, Smokey wandered to the attached room to sleep.

Suddenly, we heard the elevator door slam shut. Mike and I turned to look at each other, aghast. I wondered for a moment if maybe it was others from our crew coming to join us, but then I spotted two White Hats stepping out of the elevator with the ironworker foreman. We thought about running for the stairs but hesitated too long. Before we knew it, the White Hats were on the catwalk heading toward us. Mike recognized both White Hats and confirmed that they were important engineers.

We turned off the light and figured we would just keep quiet until the three of them were out of sight or on the platform above. Then, we'd run for the ladder. We had no phone or Bridge radio, and nobody else knew we were up there, so we would just have to patiently wait it out.

Through the cracks in the walls, we anxiously watched all that was going on outside the shack. The three of them stood around talking for a while. Then, the ironworker and one of the White Hats went to the elevator, telling the remaining White Hat that they were going up to Strut Five and would be back later to retrieve him. We just needed him to walk away; then, we could make a run for it.

This guy looked like he rarely left the office and did not have the appearance of a site engineer, which is probably why they left him behind. He checked out the area around the shack, having no idea anyone was in there, let alone watching him through the cracks. I noticed him staring at the shack door and realized we'd forgotten to use our special decoy lock, so now it was obvious that the shack was unlocked. Seeing him reach for the door,

Mike quickly grabbed the inside handle. The engineer pulled on the door, pushed it, and shook it, but he just could not understand why this unlocked door wouldn't open. Mike hung on as tightly as he could until the guy retreated at last. Then, he abruptly changed his mind and charged in again, putting his shoulder into it, but luckily Mike held. The guy was probably a brilliant engineer, but he could not figure this one out. Mike quietly secured the bolt, and we sighed with relief as he finally backed away from the now-locked door.

The White Hat then went to the tool table across from the shack, only about seven feet from us, and sat down on one of the chairs. He opened his laptop and began typing away, looking as though he'd be planted there for a while. Our escape plan was thwarted, and we were still trapped.

Smokey had been asleep in the attached room this whole time, blissfully unaware of what was happening. He had this terrible habit of letting out a loud, low-pitched, animal-like growl when waking up from a nap, and he was starting to stir.

Mike whispered, "What if Smokey wakes up and makes that stupid growl? It will be a dead giveaway we're here."

It was dark, and we had only the dim light that shone through the cracks, but I found a dirty old rag, crammed it into a glove, and held it ready over Smokey's head. "I'll jam this freaking glove in his mouth the second he starts to make that noise," I hissed. Fortunately, Smokey drifted off again, and the mouth stuffing was put on hold. I still kept the glove handy, just in case.

We watched as the White Hat got up and shook the door again. This guy wanted in the shack badly. But once he sat back down, he noticed something else that diverted his attention. It was beside the tool table in a green plastic bag. He looked at it for a few minutes and then got up for a closer inspection. He pulled the plastic down, and there it was, an old half-filled pee bottle, which must have been sitting there undisturbed for at least a year. As I peered through the cracks, I was thinking, "Dude, if you know what's best, you won't get near that thing."

His curiosity once again got the best of him, though. He just had to know what was in that bottle. We saw him flip the cap and shove his face in close, and the second he got a whiff, he did a jig that I can find only one way to describe: think of a chicken bobbing its head up and down quickly to grab seed off the ground. That is what this guy's head was doing as his nose curled up and his mouth gaped, nearly ready to puke. It was one of the funniest things I ever saw in my life. Mike and I had tears in our eyes as we struggled to keep from bursting into laughter.

He replaced the lid, then leaned over the catwalk rail, and we thought for sure he would throw up. Finally, he sat back down, wiped his forehead, and returned his focus to the unlocked shack, but the negative consequences of his last bout of curiosity kept him in place.

Smokey woke up just then, and before he could make a sound, I grabbed him and held my finger to my lips. He wanted to know what was going on, but I whispered for him to just shut up. At this point, we had been waiting two hours for the engineer to leave, and it was now after 11:00. I decided we should just walk out of there as if nothing unusual was going on. Mike smiled and shrugged in agreement.

We opened the shack door, and all three of us sauntered out, one after the other. The engineer snapped his head up, so shocked that he almost dropped his laptop. We all made for the West Side ladder, into the darkness. He looked at us, then quickly back to the door, and his eyes caught mine. As I passed him, his eyes still locked on me, I tipped my hard hat, bowed my head, said, "Good day, sir," and then made my way into the darkness and down the ladder. Mike and I were laughing uncontrollably the whole way down. Smokey was demanding to know what was so funny, but we didn't even know how to explain it to him. It was between Mike, me, and some nameless engineer, an experience none of us will forget.

I always wondered if that poor guy ever told anyone about his unforgettable morning in the strut. Could he ever tell anyone about this? About the rancid bottle of who knows what and those three guys who appeared out of nowhere?

I made sure to unlock the door to the crew shack when we left so he could go in and see that there was no trap door or any other way of entering. I can see him smiling to himself later, thinking, "I knew there was somebody in that shack. I just knew it!"

A VIEW THROUGH THE FOG

CHAPTER 16

PREVENTION PROTOCOL

Boats docked at the U.S. Coast Guard Golden Gate Station in Sausalito, always ready to rescue an unfortunate suicide jumper.

A VIEW THROUGH THE FOG

A few suicide jumpers are rescued and live, but it takes more than just luck to survive a jump from the Golden Gate Bridge. The accounts given by jump survivors all describe sincere regret setting in immediately after the jump. From this, we can assume that most of the hundreds of jumpers who were not lucky enough to survive had similar regrets.

Suicide can be attempted in many different ways, but most methods of taking one's own life are fallible. Suicide by jumping off the Golden Gate Bridge constitutes a good chance of completing the suicide, a 98% death rate, to be exact. In four seconds, it is all over. During that four-second fall, the body will travel the 240 feet at 75-80 MPH, ending with a bone-shattering impact of 15,000 pounds per square inch.

This type of fall will destroy a body, and, in most instances, will cause instant death. Those who actually survive the fall will most likely drown from asphyxiation or breathing in too much salt water as they're submerged, unconscious, in the swiftly moving 350-foot-deep channel. Those who remain conscious may succumb to extensive internal bleeding while trying to stay afloat. They may also die of shock, and if not rescued quickly, can die of hypothermia in the chilly waters.

On September 25, 2000, 19-year-old Kevin Hines took a 240-foot headfirst dive off the Bridge. During the jump, Hines had instantaneous regret and decided he wanted to live.. The US Coast Guard rescued Hines immediately. He had suffered serious spinal damage as three of his vertebrae were shattered, lacerating his lower organs, but he was alive.

Hines' regret is obvious in this heartfelt post-jump statement: "There was a millisecond of free fall. In that instant, I thought, 'What have I just done? I don't want to die. God, please save me.'" Hines has since regained full mobility. He is an advocate for mental health and the prevention of Bridge suicides and has written an enormously popular book about his suicide attempt called *Cracked, Not Broken*, and he directed and produced a film chronicling his journey called *Suicide The Ripple Effect*.

I remember another jumper and his amazing feat of survival. On March 10, 2011, a report came over our Bridge radios that a man held onto the outer chord after climbing over the rail at the south end of the Bridge between the South Tower and the South Anchor Block. Later, we would find out that the jumper was Luke Vilagomez, a 17-year-old from Windsor, California, on a field trip with his high school class.

I leaned over the rail and saw the teen dangling above an area where local surfing enthusiasts sometimes spend their lunch hour catching a few waves. Vilagomez eventually let go, falling into the water and landing near a group of these surfers. One of them, 55-year-old Frederic Lecoutier, had an extensive medical background and helped the injured teen to shore. Lecoutier resuscitated Vilagomez, saving his life. He'd broken his coccyx and punctured a lung, but he survived. The teen later claimed that he jumped for "fun" and not suicide, but whatever the reason, his story serves as a good example of what I mean when I say a jumper sometimes needs to be more than just lucky to survive a jump.

There is also the unusual case of Paul Aladdin Alarab from Kensington, in the East Bay, who miraculously survived a fall from the Bridge in 1988. As an act of protest against what he believed to be the mistreatment of the elderly and the handicapped, Alarab lowered himself into a garbage can that hung from the Bridge on a 60-foot rope. He lost his grip on the rope and fell. He suffered three broken ribs, and both lungs collapsed, but he survived. Alarab told the *San Francisco Chronicle*, "It seemed like the fall lasted forever. I was praying for God to give me another chance. I was also wondering about how I would hit [the water], because that is what determines if you will live or die." This incident was considered an accident, not a suicide.

However, 15 years later, Alarab again found himself in a compromising situation at the Bridge. On March 19, 2003, the now-44-year-old Alarab, protesting the US invasion of Iraq, tied one end of a rope to the outer rail, and the other he wrapped around his arms, Then, he climbed over the rail at mid-span, dangling below the outer chord. Alarab read a statement he had written denouncing the war while law enforcement tried to talk him back over the railing. After finishing the statement, he let go of the rope and fell to the waters below. This time he did not survive, and investigators ruled this incident a suicide. I guess beating the odds of surviving a fall from the Golden Gate Bridge was not enough for Alarab.

Various methods have been tried to reduce the number of suicides. Suicide hotline telephones are installed across the Bridge, and staff regularly patrol the Bridge in carts or on bicycles, looking for people who appear to be planning to jump. In addition to the Golden Gate Bridge Patrol, law enforcement and emergency medical personnel, Bridge Management takes pride in training employees from other departments in suicide prevention.

Golden Gate Bridge ironworkers and painters volunteer their time to prevent suicides and receive training on the various signs to look for when someone is in crisis, ways to engage people walking alone on the Bridge, and safety protocol when approaching a suspicious person who requires police intervention. These tactics have helped convince many people not to take their own lives.

California Highway Patrol officer Kevin Briggs is credited with saving the lives of hundreds of would-be jumpers by talking them out of jumping. The CHP estimates that with the help of cameras and volunteers, at least 80-90% of people intending to jump are prevented from doing so. But sometimes all the training in the world is not enough, and just being yourself and lending an ear to someone in distress can be the remedy.

It was a blustery day on the Bridge. A woman had climbed over the guardrail and stood upon the outer chord below. Scared and trembling, she clung tightly to the Bridge support cables that ran up through the chord, threatening to let go if anyone tried to grab her.

Alfredo, a Bridge painter working nearby, calmly approached the frightened young lady. He sat beside her for over an hour, and through a dialogue full of heartfelt concern and patience, Alfredo eventually talked this desperate person out of jumping and then helped her back over the rail to safety.

The crowd that had gathered around to anxiously watch the incident play out, which included myself, began cheering as Alfredo helped the woman into the Bridge Patrol scooter that would take her off the Bridge alive. For this woman, the odds of remaining alive are good. A study of people stopped from jumping off the Golden Gate Bridge, started in 1978, found that 94% were still alive more than 26 years later. It was a glorious achievement on Alfredo's part, and for his act of caring, the Golden Gate Bridge Board awarded him Bridge District Employee of the Year. There is now one more person in this world with a second chance at a happy life, thanks to Alfredo.

Not all Bridge employees have had compassion for suicide jumpers. Some have rationalized letting someone who wants to jump do so. Others were just not interested either way. Then, there were those who actually found a way to capitalize on and derive amusement from another's tragedy.

The Golden Gate Bridge, like work places all across America, has seen many types of gambling among its employees. Poker games, dominoes, football pools, parlay cards—basically, any type of gambling that could exist, did. Management frowned on gambling in the workplace, but hey, good luck trying to eliminate it.

One enterprising employee took workplace gambling to its lowest possible level with a "jumper pool." The format was a monthly calendar with blank squares for each day of the month. A participant paid for a square, then chose any day on the calendar and signed his name, initials, or alias. If a suicide occurred on the day he chose, he won all the money built up since the day of the last jump. If there were no jumps during that month, the pot rolled over to the next month.

I viewed this pool as just a bad joke or a novelty that would soon go away. However, it did not just go away. In fact, the first month's sheet filled up so fast that another pool for the month was added. A small number of employees took part in this pool while most others thought it to be irresponsible and in poor taste. The players were not necessarily evil people; they were just among those who had no compassion for jumpers or those with a serious gambling addiction.

Not much mystery surrounded the identities of those in the pool. They were usually the ones running to Bridge security first thing in the morning to ask if there had been any jumpers the day before. Every time someone jumped, I could not avoid the thought that a fellow worker had just made some money. I couldn't imagine someone actually hoping a person would jump off the Bridge on a particular day, just to make a few dollars, but I guess we are all different people.

The pool discreetly flourished for a few months. Eventually, good judgment won out, and interest waned. Bridge Management learned of the pool's existence, and horrified, they immediately laid down a zero-tolerance rule. Anyone found to be involved in these games would be unconditionally terminated. Management also punished the rest of us by banning all types of gambling and wagering. Collateral damage can be a motivational force, and at that point the rest of the department rose up against the abhorrent pool and put a swift end to it. Eventually, our football pools and card games resurfaced, but I want to believe that the jumper pool will stay gone forever.

Management took great pains to ensure that we made it to the end of each day still alive. As high steel painters, we spent many hours training to work safely. We were required to always work in pairs, assuring mutual safety. We could never know when a life-threatening situation involving a fellow worker might arise but had to be prepared if it did. We didn't always get along with one another, but this was okay because when things went bad, we definitely had each other's backs, as this next account will illustrate.

Driving southbound toward San Francisco in the far lane next to the West Sidewalk, a man abruptly stopped his car, jumped out, and climbed through the safety barrier onto the sidewalk. As pointed out before, this sidewalk is for Bridge worker access only and off-limits to tourists, but concern for such trivial restrictions seemed meaningless to this man.

I was driving my paint scooter down the East Sidewalk when I saw the man stop his car and run for the West Sidewalk. A large commotion began, highlighted by skidding tires and honking horns as cars swerved to miss the abandoned vehicle. This man, like the woman jumper I mentioned earlier, had his mind made up that he wanted over the rail, into the water, and out of his life.

Things were happening so quickly that there was no way Bridge security would get to this man before he could jump. Once he entered the sidewalk, I saw that the man was heading toward one of our paint scooters parked near the South Tower. Two painters sat in the parked scooter, Junior in the cab and Mar in the back.

The jumper made for the outer rail at the South Tower. Spotting him, Mar leaped out of the scooter and got into position to intercept him before he could get to the rail. Just a few steps away from Mar, the man surprised us all when he took the car keys that he held in his hand and threw them as hard as he could into Mar's face. Mar clutched his face in pain. The chaos did not stop here. Instead of side-stepping the stunned painter and continuing with his jump, this tall, well-built man used all his heightened anxiety to run straight into Mar, slamming him hard against the outer rail. The larger man grabbed Mar's right leg and began trying to force the shocked painter over the rail.

This all happened in a matter of seconds. I watched in amazement and horror, helpless on the other side of the roadway, as a co-worker struggled for his life against a madman. The man lifted Mar's right leg even higher, causing his left leg to rise off the ground too. I remember thinking that Mar might actually be thrown over the rail.

Then, out of nowhere, Junior came up behind the crazed man and grabbed him around the neck, causing the man to release Mar, who fell to the sidewalk. Junior wrestled the would-be jumper to the ground, mashing the man's face against the sidewalk. The man still violently protested, but Junior's strength kept him pinned to the ground until more help arrived.

Witnessing this bizarre chain of events left me feeling as though I had just watched a scene from an action movie. Junior saved his partner when the opportunity presented itself, and it served as a good example of why we work in pairs. An ever-thankful Mar made sure Junior did not have to worry about buying his own lunch for a long time after that. Junior's quick reaction not only saved his partner's life but the life of the potential jumper as well. I'll never know how this new chance at life affected the redeemed jumper, but he will have to deal with being alive for a while longer and hopefully make the most of his new opportunity. Staying alive was our number-one priority at the Bridge, and all three of these men made it to the end of that day because of Junior.

The US Coast Guard is on constant alert for jumpers. When a person is seen jumping from the sidewalk, they will be first responders to the scene. US Coast Guard Station Golden Gate is in Sausalito at Fort Baker on Horseshoe Bay, located under the Bridge near the North End. The station has two 47-foot motor lifeboats. When someone jumps from the Golden Gate Bridge, one of these two boats can get to the scene in 4-5 minutes with sailors who retrieve the jumper and perform lifesaving measures.

Spotting a body can be difficult at eye level from a Coast Guard rescue vessel. As soon as a jump is confirmed, Bridge Patrol will navigate to where the jump occurred, exit onto the sidewalk through the access gate, and immediately drop a smoke flare (which is basically a smoking kettle, the size of a basketball) straight down into the water, from the spot the jump was made.

The jumper's body will sometimes be submerged several feet below the surface and start drifting even before the Coast Guard can get to the scene. The smoking flare will drift the same route as the body whether the tide is ebbing or flowing inward. This way, the Coast Guard can follow the rising smoke to locate the body quickly. This will give the Coast Guard a better chance at a rescue.

The Coast Guard is ready to respond quickly to revive a drowning victim, administer CPR to an injured survivor, and get a potential survivor out of the water before hypothermia sets in. Unfortunately, however, most cases end with the grim task of locating and removing a lifeless body from the water.

The Bridge has an efficient Suicide Prevention Response Plan. While the US Coast Guard are the first responders when a jumper hits the water, other measures are in place to prevent a prospective jumper from getting that far.

The first level of jump prevention is a trained Bridge security team, capable of responding quickly to any type of suicide jumper threat. For urgent cases, Bridge Patrol vehicles teamed with Bridge tow service can create a lane diversion or closure to quickly converge on a possible jumper, who can then be questioned or escorted from the Bridge to a safer place to talk further with Bridge officials. For questionable, less obvious suspects who may only be contemplating a jump, security has officers in patrol scooters and on bicycles who can discreetly approach a suspected jumper for a more subdued encounter.

Because of the Bridge's status as an American icon, it is considered a possible target for a terrorist attack. Since 9/11, security on the Bridge has become a top priority, and as a result, the high-tech security now in place adds an additional dimension to suicide prevention. Bridge security can monitor the Bridge much more thoroughly due to dozens of security cameras that have been installed on or around the Bridge over the past decade. From a main security room, suspicious characters are now watched much more closely not only potential terrorists, but also suicide suspects. This has given Bridge Security another tool in its suicide prevention arsenal.

Another effective aspect of the Suicide Prevention Response Plan is an early warning system, that is implemented when there has been a report from a family member or loved one that someone may be heading to the Bridge with the intent to commit suicide. In these instances, Bridge security sends out a message over the Bridge radio that generally describes the person's physical characteristics, what he or she may be wearing, and even a description of the vehicle the person may be driving. This way, if Bridge workers come into contact with the person, they can inform security.

The last type of suicide prevention uses a more hand on approach, primarily involving Bridge ironworkers and painters since they frequent the sidewalks all day. They carry Bridge radios and have the authority to report any suspicious people they observe to Bridge security. Of course, there is also the option of approaching possible jumpers and talking with them to determine what their intentions might be. To judge whether a person may or may not be contemplating suicide is more often than not a tough call as was the case with Alfredo.

Proponents of a suicide barrier have long argued that the Golden Gate Bridge's popular legend, coupled with its easy access and relatively low safety rail, makes it a prime destination for those contemplating suicide. Barriers on the Eiffel Tower and Empire State Building have been successful in deterring jumpers. Anti-suicide and mental health activists have pressured Bridge directors for decades to create some sort of suicide barrier for the Bridge.

Bridge officials are sympathetic to the grief that families of suicide victims endure. I have attended Golden Gate Bridge and Transportation District Board public meetings and witnessed victims' family members questioning whether their loved ones would have committed suicide had they not been drawn to the Bridge's easy access to a jump.

On October 10, 2008, the Golden Gate Bridge Board of Directors voted 15-1 to install a stainless-steel net as a suicide deterrent at a cost initially estimated at $40-50 million. In 2010, the board received $5 million from the Metropolitan Transportation Commission (MTC) for a final design study of the barrier.

Funding for the overall project had still not been secured, causing concern that this lack of money would delay the project. However, funds for the building of the barrier were unanimously approved by the board on June 27, 2014. The MTC, along with federal and state grants, Bridge tolls, and donations from both individuals and foundations would contribute to the now-estimated $76 million price tag. Finally, construction could begin on the netting to deter suicide jumps.

The community-selected design was chosen for its proven effectiveness and its minimalist aesthetics. The completed Suicide Deterrent Net System (SDNS) will comprise 385,000 square feet of marine-grade stainless steel netting attached to 369 structural steel net supports placed 20 feet below the sidewalk and extending out 20 feet over the water. The metal support beams will then be installed first and painted International Orange.

The metal net and border cables will be installed and remain gray to blend in with the ocean water below.

Another major change will be required to successfully install the new SDNS system. For decades, painters and ironworkers have used combustion engine powered travelers to do maintenance work on the structure beneath the Bridge. These motorized scaffolds, or travelers, wrap around the sides of the Bridge and pass along its underside. Due to the new SDNS, the travelers will need to be removed, and replaced with smaller electric units. New railings must be installed to allow the travelers to move along the side of the Bridge.

"This is the largest suicide deterrent net installation in the world, especially in the country," said Ewa Bauer-Furbush, the Bridge's Chief Engineer. "It is a technically complex project that requires a lot of effort from all vendors of the project team that are involved in bringing this to completion."

Fabrication of the steel netting began off-site in May 2017, and installation of the netting began onsite in August 2018. The netting had originally been set for completion in 2021, but now delays have extended the completion date to 2023 and ballooned the final cost to $211 million.

Responsibility for the delay rests solely on the company contracted for the construction of the net. Shimmick Construction in joint venture with Danny's Construction submitted the low bid and were awarded the contract, but with construction on the net barely having commenced, AECOM purchased Shimmick. The distraction brought confusion and disorganization to the project.

A frustrated Denis Mulligan, the Golden Gate Bridge General Manager, described what he believed to be the reasons for the delay. "AECOM was slow to mobilize on the job site. They lagged in building temporary construction platforms beneath the span, and the company presented an optimistic timeline that didn't pan out, underestimating the time needed to complete certain steps."

The delay also frustrated the backers of the suicide barrier because 26 people died after jumping from the Bridge in 2019. This means that delays with the Suicide Safety Net may lead to 20-30 deaths each year by suicide until the net is completed. It is now 2023, and the safety net is facing still more delays as the bottom traveler scaffold system is showing severe deterioration due to excessive rust. The Bridge continues to work hard to remedy this situation.

A VIEW THROUGH THE FOG

CHAPTER 17

THE NAV PROJECT

The sandblast platform containment at the North Approach Viaduct (NAV) kept paint crews busy for years and the environment free from contamination.

A VIEW THROUGH THE FOG

During my seventh year at the Bridge, the North Approach Viaduct (NAV) project got underway. As mentioned earlier, it required sandblasting and painting a quarter-mile stretch at the approach to the North End of the Bridge under the roadway in a fully contained work environment. After years of preparation, this enormous project was finally ready to start. At the same time, a private engineering firm was working on a massive retrofit job in the North Anchor Block. With these two projects going on simultaneously, the North End of the Bridge inevitably became one huge, hectic job site.

The NAV project was now the Paint Department's number-one priority. Due to attrition, the original five paint crews had been reduced to three. The Boneyard crew and another crew had been lost, leaving two large crews that would sandblast on the NAV project and one smaller crew to do any other jobs on the Bridge.

A work site with the look of a small shantytown had been set up beneath the approach at the North End. Our sandblast equipment, compressors, and vacuum system, along with everything else required to operate the job, were in place. Sharing this site with us was a crew of ironworkers who would construct our containment area and build the work platform above. A crew of operating engineers was assigned with supplying our air, maintaining the sandblast and vacuum units, and regulating our ventilation in the containments. The two paint crews had a trailer stationed at the operation site, as did these two support crews. Such close proximity to specialists in other trades (especially those who had never been shy about expressing their envy of and contempt for our unorthodox work practices and high pay rate) meant even further scrutinizing of our egregious ways.

The NAV job differed from anything than we had done in a long time, not so much in the work itself but in how we went about doing it. The rules had changed. Expectations had changed. We had lost our cherished freedoms and now found ourselves under the microscope.

Over the past year, management had incorporated new work guidelines that took away nearly all our privileges. We were to ride to the North End in a crew van every morning at 7:00 a.m. and would not return to the Toll Plaza yard until 3:00 p.m. This eliminated our two hours per day of leisure time, to which we had become very accustomed. Asking us to work eight hours instead of six and be paid the same? How dare they!

Of course, they were just expecting us to comply with commonplace work methods practiced everywhere every day, but to a group of prima donna painters at the Golden Gate Bridge, this was like a shot to the heart. I am ashamed and embarrassed now to admit that I, too, pouted a little about the new expectations. Yet, I realized that whether I liked it or not, change was inevitable. Some other painters could not see the writing on the wall, and their shortsightedness and obstinacy just made us look even sillier. Our power had dwindled, and management, with the help of a few other trades, was going to use our own arrogance against us.

As I mentioned before, cameras had been placed in many locations on and around the Bridge. The official reason for this was, of course, that the Golden Gate Bridge was a high-profile national monument and a potential terrorist target.

But Bridge security personnel were not the only ones with access to these cameras. Bridge Maanagement had access as well, with large viewing monitors in their offices that could show many locations at once, or combine several individual camera views into a large projection. They assured us that the cameras were not being used to view Bridge employees at work, but just to be on the safe side, if we spotted one that looked to be pointed at us, we knew to at least try to look like we were working.

Some could be operated remotely by security or anybody with access, changing the direction of the camera from wherever they were viewing. It was not uncommon to see a camera on a light pole suddenly maneuver up and down or side to side, looking for a better view. At times, a group of painters might have been loitering during work hours only to notice a camera begin to revolve on its turret and then stop when it was directly aimed at them, wordlessly telling them it was time to break up the party.

Eventually, we got a chance to see just how effective a camera, or even the suggestion of a camera, could be in the workplace. A painter had put a box containing 100 lumpia in the break-room freezer. He complained that someone kept stealing his lumpia, but since painters were in and out of the break room all day, he had no way of knowing who might be the thief.

In the ceiling of this room, an access opening had had several missing panels for as long as I could remember. One day, one of the painters spotted what appeared to be a camera mounted up inside this hole, pointed at the freezer. We'd never noticed it before and wondered where in the heck it had come from, but since we were just there to eat and had nothing to hide, we soon lost interest in it.

I guess the one who had been taking the lumpia did not lose interest, however, because the guy who'd complained of his food being stolen mentioned later that the theft had stopped. He attributed it to that camera. Months later, we finally decided to give the camera a closer inspection, so a painter climbed up and brought it down for us. It turned out to be a Pop-Tart box wrapped in black electrical tape with a camera lens taped to the end. But it had worked! Just the appearance of a surveillance camera was enough to deter the "lumpia bandit."

Then, there was the matter of the North End tourist parking lot. Painters had long been parking their personal vehicles here instead of in the employee parking lot at the Toll Plaza. This way, they could jump into their cars at any time of day without worrying about being seen by Bridge personnel and then head on home, having someone else sign them out. A short time after the cameras had been installed, a memo came from Bridge Management: it had come to their attention that painters were leaving early in their personal vehicles, and anyone caught doing this would be severely punished. We assumed management had seen painters leaving on film, but at that point, it didn't matter whether or not they were actually watching us. The knowledge that half a dozen light poles at the North End had cameras mounted on them was deterrent enough. *Big Brother* was watching—maybe, and in this new age of Bridge painter accountability, the cameras at the North End were efficient weapons.

Sandblasting was the most physical part of our job. Hanging onto a hard rubber hose only 2" in diameter, while over a hundred pounds of continuous air pressure pushes sand through it and then out of a 6" tungsten-lined blast nozzle, is not easy. There can be no mistakes or mishandling of the hose. Dropping it could cause injury to you or anyone near you. To make things even more difficult, much of the blasting is done while carefully balancing yourself on narrow scaffold planks 10-15 feet above the platform floor.

While sandblasting, we wore heavy-duty protective gear to deflect the sand and rust that would ricochet off the steel directly onto one's face, body, and hands. Getting geared up to sandblast was like suiting up for battle. We wore hard plastic air-fed hoods with replaceable plastic face shields, thick rubber pants and jackets, leather welding gloves for our hands, and ear plugs or muffs inside our helmets to lessen the deafening sound of the air and sand whistling through the nozzle.

Despite all the protective gear, getting accidentally shot, or "peppered," by other sandblasters was painful, even from as far as 30 feet away. Placing four painters in the containment, blasting steel from many different directions, often caused a sand crossfire, and getting peppered with sand was just something you had to deal with.

Twenty years earlier, while working for a contractor, I'd found out the hard way how painful and dangerous sandblasting could be. I was shot point-blank in my side from about two feet away by another's blast hose. I did not realize the extent of my injury until I looked down and saw my shirt saturated with blood. Fifteen minutes later, the numbness of the shock wore off, and I felt the most horrible stinging pain I had ever felt in my life. This was nothing compared to the pain that came later when a doctor spent two hours tweezing out all the sand that had lodged in my flesh, one granule at a time. I almost passed out from the pain, and I am not ashamed to say that I cried like a baby that night. Forever afterward, I respected sandblasting for the injuries it could inflict, and I have a large scar to prove it.

Sandblast peppering might just be part of the job, but when a shot of sand from a blast hose whacks you unexpectedly, that split-second rush of pain really smarts and can sure piss you off.

One morning, four of us were set to blast. We each had our own designated area of steel to blast within the containment, and we got the ground man's hand signal to start. The instant my blaster switched on, I got peppered with sand in my back. I winced behind my helmet but remained calm, shut off my blaster, and turned to look around me. I couldn't see any other blasters pointed in my direction although Smokey was busy blasting just to my right.

I shrugged it off and resumed blasting. Again, I got peppered in the back. This time it was even more painful. I shut down and looked around again. Still, nobody was aiming their blaster in my direction. I narrowed my eyes at Smokey, who gave me a goofy smile through the shield of his helmet.

I wondered what in the heck was going on. I started up my blasting and for the third time got shot in the back. I shut down, spun quickly around, and saw Smokey still looking at me. I figured it had to be him. I waved my arms frantically, cussing at him inside my helmet, to which, of course, he indicated he had no idea what I was saying. He stopped his blasting and shrugged his shoulders as if he could not understand why I was so mad.

I turned away, flustered and red-faced, thinking to myself, "Okay, I just know this idiot is blasting me in the back every time I turn around. If he does it again, I'm going to get him."

I switched my blaster on, and sure enough, I was peppered right in the small of my back again. That was it! I swung around and pointed my blaster at the steel surface Smokey was working on. I bounced the sand off the steel towards him, and I could see through his face shield that his eyes were popping out of his head. He jumped off his stage and ran as I shot sand around him until he was 50 feet away.

While I was busy shooting Smokey with sand, I gradually realized that I was also still being pelted, even with Smokey gone. I looked down, confused, and immediately knew who the true idiot was—me. My blast hose had a hole worn through it about 15 feet back (holes in hoses was not uncommon), but the fact that this hole had been angled right up toward my back was against all odds. Every time I faced the steel and switched on, I was getting peppered by my own hose, and every time I let off the trigger and turned around, it would stop.

Poor Smokey must have thought I was a psycho when I snapped and started blasting him. I always hated having to apologize to this man who had no shame, but this time I had no choice but to be humbled and not only tell him I was sorry for blasting him but also admit that I'd actually been blasting myself the whole time!

Our South Tower crew was the only crew that had sandblasted on the Bridge in the past ten years. Most other painters had not blasted in over a decade, while some never had at all.

With the new painter accountability factors set in place on the NAV project, we would be required to blast several hours a day, which was certainly more blasting than even we were accustomed to. Our crew was at least experienced, somewhat warmed up, and ready to take on this new project, but some of the old-time painters from other crews were not quite up for the challenge.

Some of these veterans gave sandblasting a try, but the physical demands were too much. With no Boneyard crew to offer refuge, half a dozen painters who had put in enough years called it quits. They retired peacefully, thus avoiding the impending physical and mental stress that was staring them in the face.

It was time to bring in some new painters. These would be the Department's first new painters since I had been hired eight years earlier. Eight new hires trickled in over the next couple of years. Most of them had worked together before coming to the Bridge, and I had worked with many of them on other jobs prior to my Bridge days.

Just as it had been for me when I started, some of these new painters had lots of questions and struggled to understand our ways. I tried to give them some of the same advice I'd gotten. I told them to relax and forget all they ever knew about painting because it would be different here. I reassured them they were in a better place. This did not seem to be enough for them. They were different, and times were different.

When I had started at the Bridge years before, painters ruled the roost. The perks were amazing, and I could do the job at my own pace and sink into occupational bliss. The fundamental difference between then and now was that while I'd been hired to be a worker, they were hired to work.

The new painters had heard all the stories before they got to the Bridge, and they couldn't wait to start making a lot of money and enjoy great benefits while working at a nice easy pace. This was not to be. Instead, they were hired with a much less lucrative retirement plan and without the "Cadillac" health benefit package that we had enjoyed for so many years. It was a different place altogether for new hires.

They were also immediately stationed at the NAV project site with a sandblast hose in their hands. Because most had done little sandblasting before, this was a rude awakening, nothing like what they had imagined the job to be. But there was no turning back.

Most of the new painters assumed the stories they had heard about "shacks" and "downtime" were nothing more than rumors, so they never really knew what they had missed. Others thought differently. They knew the stories were true and were aware of what had been taken away from us. To them, we were lazy, bumbling fools, and they became resentful of us, feeling as though they were being punished for our past mistakes. As true as this may have been, it was a cup half-empty kind of outlook because they still had the best painting job in existence.

I felt sorry for what the new painters would never know. They'd never seen a painters' shack; had never met the Boneyard crew; and had never been in a Tower elevator. I wouldn't even have known how to begin telling them about the crew shack in Strut Four or a pee bucket. On second thought, perhaps they were better off not knowing, whereas I had known and lost.

The new recruits mirrored my own soul. As I knew most of them already, it was nice to greet them as they came aboard. There was lots of genial banter and remarks about how gray my hair was or how big my belly had gotten, but what really hit home were the comments about how much my work ethic had changed and how it seemed I was in early retirement mode. Okay, I got that, but it still stung.

I took pride in helping to ease them into their new job, but in the end, it was actually they who helped me. I realized some things about myself; I was reminded of what it was like just starting out on the Bridge. I had wanted to be a Golden Gate Bridge painter so much, to work on the Bridge and be a part of something special. My good intentions had seemed so wonderful, but somewhere along the way things changed. I had become mesmerized by the perks and the downtime, and I became bitter with resentment when they were taken away. I was fighting an enemy that did not exist, and I was no longer thankful for what I had. Our claim that we were just products of our environment only served as a hollow excuse. We were drawn in by tradition and tempted by human nature.

By then, it was the early 2000s, and the world around us was evolving. Long-overdue social changes were finally being realized. Environmental concerns, diversity awareness, inclusion, coping with stress, and empathy were some of the issues becoming more relevant across the country. Gradually, these changes would be incorporated into the American workplace and ultimately make their way to the Golden Gate Bridge Paint Department.

When it came to our outdated work traditions, we were obstinate and unyielding to the changes that Bridge Management was trying to force upon us, but social change was different—universally embraced and barrelling toward us at breakneck speed. We had no choice but to hop aboard this one or else be crushed beneath the wheels of change.

How would a bunch of salty old painters take to lowering the shields that protected our entitled privileges and freedoms? As it turned out, the majority of painters were on board. I mean, we were still human beings, and most of the new changes were predicated on treating those around you with respect and awareness. Still, you know what they say about teaching old dogs new tricks.

Look at us, entering the 21st century! By the time I had retired, the paint department had taken on a new look. A more refined look. Jokes had a less offensive veneer; the amount of playful hazing and bullying dwindled; and horseplay was limited. We still argued, but arguments never ended in physical confrontation. Maybe a work environment was not meant to resemble an old-time western saloon after all.

As I was nearing the end of my painting career, I remembered something I used to tell myself years ago when things at my job would get me down: "The worst thing they can possibly do is make me work eight hours a day and pay me for eight hours a day, and how bad is that?"

I experienced a resurgence of pride and enthusiasm in my last year on the Bridge. Perhaps this arose from my desire to convince the new hires that I was still every bit the painter I always had been. Or maybe I had resensed my obligation to care for this extraordinary structure so that she might stand forever, a duty I'd embraced with enthusiasm when hired years before. For whatever reason, I sandblasted until my last day on the Bridge and got to leave the trade my way, working strong until the end.

The North Approach project took over five years to complete. Sadly, I would work on that project until I retired and never had another task on the Bridge itself. I knew how I would miss the East Sidewalk, the tourists, the cool breeze, the smell of the ocean, and all the wonderful things that made working there so enjoyable.

CHAPTER 18

LAST GOODBYE

foghorn standing guard on the South Tower Pier, always ready to warm of dangerous fog in the shipping lanes

A VIEW THROUGH THE FOG

The morning forecast of fog had put our North Approach sandblast job on hold until after first break. With our shacks a thing of the distant past, we would be expected to wait out the inclement weather at the contained work site as a group. As I headed to my scooter in the maintenance yard, I overheard a paint laborer being assigned the task of exchanging all the fire extinguishers in the South Tower for freshly charged ones. A thought came to mind that the couple hours of down-time made this a perfect opportunity for me to do some long overdue sightseeing.

I ran to the laborer's scooter as he pulled away, beating hard on the side box with my palms to get his attention. The scooter abruptly stopped, causing the couple dozen fire extinguishers in the back to clang together noisily. He gladly accommodated my request to go along. My impulsive offer to help with the extinguishers was not exactly what I had planned, but it would get me to my destination.

A thick wall of fog engulfed the towers, causing the main cables to nearly disappear, nothing more than their bottom curve at mid-span exposed. The scooter's lone wiper squeaked across the windshield, and beads of moisture streamed along the side passenger window as we motored down the East Sidewalk. The thick blanket of fog above us would soon envelop the sidewalk, becoming denser as clusters of fog hitched rides on the choppy breezes drifting across the Bridge. After we unloaded the fire extinguishers at the tower, the laborer went off to park his scooter. I walked to the observation sidewalk that rounded the tower. Looking down past the safety rail, I could see more fog rolling across the water in large clumps from the sea, but not nearly as thick as it was above.

Bridge security arrived to unlock the tower doors for us. We moved half a dozen extinguishers into the elevator and left the others in the narrow entryway. After shutting the main door, we climbed aboard the tiny elevator. Two riders cramped the elevator cage enough, but the addition of six fire extinguishers made things even more awkward. Once inside, we maneuvered into separate corners, attempting to straddle the extinguishers. I slid the elevator's laced metal screen door closed, and we were ready to depart.

Before lifting the lever, though, the laborer said, "Hey, you don't have to help me with this. It's probably easier if I do it myself." Then, he added, "I can drop you off anywhere you want to go."

"That would be real cool." I nodded respectfully.

"You want me to take you to the top?" he asked, ready to raise the lever.

"Top of the tower," I thought to myself. Perhaps the most beautiful view in the world. I'd spent many hours having my mind blown in its remarkable presence. I knew this morning's fog would surely put a damper on the view but not its gifts of reflection and wonder. But this was not my destination today.

"Not today." I said emphatically, "Would you take me down to the pier?"

"Sure. You can drop off a couple of extinguishers while you're down there."

The South Tower Pier had always been my favorite place at the Bridge. It had been at least six years since I'd been down there. I really missed it, but I figured there would always be time to say one last goodbye. This was that time.

An earthquake retrofit project had been scheduled for the South Tower soon, and the pier would then be off-limits to Bridge workers. With my tenure at the Bridge ending in a matter of weeks, this would be my last opportunity to visit the pier. Anticipation swelled in my chest as the elevator started its slow descent.

The fire extinguishers wobbled and clanked, creating an eerie echo throughout the dark, cavernous shaft. A slight chill came over me, as this echo seemed somehow different. I felt as though we were descending through a soulless shell. For years, the tower had been a bustling sanctuary for painters, whether we were working on the pier or lounging in our struts. Shaft doors would open and close at random, bells rang for the elevators, and even in complete silence, you could still sense life in the towers. Today, though, the tower felt empty. Not even the ghosts of past painters that I had sworn I'd heard and seen roamed the tower these days.

The elevator came to an abrupt stop at the bottom. I slid the metal screen to the side, unlatched the elevator shaft door, and set two extinguishers in the corridor.

"I'll be back in about a half hour, after I drop off all the extinguishers in the tower," the laborer told me, "I'll just yell from the elevator when I get back."

I saluted, then turned and began traversing the dimly lit thirty-foot corridor that led to the outer door. Stopping in the cell where Smokey had drenched our crew from above years before, I looked up, shook my head, and proceeded. Upon reaching the outer door, I grabbed the Bridge radio that was strapped around my neck and shoulders. "South Tower to security," I spoke into the radio. "Painter entering South Tower Pier."

"10-4, South Tower," came the response.

Standing at the door, I took in a deep breath, not knowing what to expect. I unlatched the door, pushed it open, and ducked through the portal.

I stood atop the metal platform, ten feet above the deck of the pier, and felt as though I was home, wishing for time to just stop. I closed my eyes and released a breath I had unconsciously been holding. A long stream of white smoke drifted from my pursed lips, and I followed this with a slow consistent inhale of the moist air that was all around me, absorbing this moment into my lungs, my bones, my senses, my memory.

The fog was less dense than it had been up on the roadway, but it was blowing in from the sea in large, scattered patches like a great herd of white mares charging toward the Bridge atop the turbulent ocean waters. I descended the metal ladder to the massive concrete deck of the pier. Work had halted on the pier since my crew had done jobs there nearly a decade before, but reminders of our time were scattered across the deck: abandoned swing stages awkwardly leaned against the towers, bereft of the long cables that had once hung them majestically from the road deck; a row of rolled-up air lines hung at eye level from the catwalks, cracked and obviously unable to hold air anymore, their original bright red color faded to a light pink hue from the years of exposure.

One thing remained intact, taking the form of an unforgettable smell that suddenly assaulted me. Shaking my head, I let out an involuntary, "Whew!" It was seagull crap.

Seagulls had commandeered the pier for their own. I guess somebody had to be the boss on the pier. If nobody else was going to step up, the seagulls would.

A few years earlier, one of the White Hats had a brilliant idea to keep the gulls away. He proposed a scarecrow-type scenario to create the illusion that a predator was constantly guarding the pier. A life-sized plastic alligator head was lowered into the waters of the moat that surrounded the pier and anchored there, giving the impression that the body attached to this fearsome-looking head was submerged in the moat, ready to attack any birds that came near.

The idea was probably researched and well thought out, but maybe someone should have informed these gulls that they were supposed to fear a predator species whose nearest non-plastic relative was thousands of miles away. Might as well have been a giant floating yard gnome.

At the edge of the pier, I looked down into the moat and noticed a group of gulls floating near the alligator and then couldn't help but laugh upon seeing a gull proudly standing on top of the plastic head. The gulls I'd previously met on the pier had an innate ability to outsmart the humans they encountered. Why would things be different with this alligator?

I looked around at all the gulls standing at attention, guarding the pier and its waters. Their white feathers rippled in the soft breeze. None looked toward me, pretending not to notice my presence, but I sensed their attention on me. They were watching. I thought perhaps they might even miss my crew and the excitement of our futile attempts to run them from the pier. Do seagulls even live that long? I wondered.

Reaching into the pocket of my coveralls, I pulled out a sausage biscuit I was saving for later, crumbled it in my hands, and tossed the broken pieces into the water near the disembodied alligator head. Birds immediately began flying in from all around the moat to get a piece of this action. Suddenly, a sea of white wings and feathers, speckled with squawking orange beaks, created a violent tumult of frothing white water. The plastic alligator head was bobbing frantically from side to side amidst the commotion, enduring a relentless beating. Within seconds, the chaos subdued, and the birds were once again floating listlessly on the water's surface as if nothing at all had happened. Yep, the seagulls had missed me, and the unfortunate alligator had become nothing more than an eyesore in the moat, waiting for its day to be retired to the Boneyard with all the other Bridge relics.

I leaned against the west rail of the pier and watched the remaining gulls as they rested on the water. Mounted on the tower at eye level a few feet to my left was the iconic Golden Gate Bridge foghorn. What I'd have given to hear the foghorn blast one last time. There's nothing quite like that brief, majestic roar bellowing across the water. But not from here, not this close. I knew from experience that at this distance, a foghorn blast meant to be heard from miles away would certainly be a head ringer or perhaps a lot worse without earplugs in place. The convergence of the humid sea air and the colder coastal waters continued to push an unrelenting wall of fog forward through the Gate, so I thought it prudent to move away from the horn.

I walked around the West leg to the center of the pier, where I stopped to reflect. I knew this would probably be my last trip to the pier, so I willed my senses to open, wanting to take in as much of this special place as possible in the short time that remained. The fog's slow, forceful descent had nearly engulfed the entire Bridge. Even the mighty tower legs that now surrounded me on both sides had succumbed to the fog, producing steady streams of moisture beads that flowed down their sides as the tower continued to slowly disappear.

The entire city of San Francisco, as well as its nearby northern shoreline, had completely disappeared from view. I had to refocus my eyes just to see Fort Point less than a quarter mile away through the thick gray wall. The faint sounds of vehicles traveling across the Bridge a couple hundred feet above and the waves splashing against the walls of the pier somewhere below me were the only indicators that I wasn't stranded on an island of nothingness.

There was no maritime activity in the waters surrounding the pier today. No elegant sailboats, no joyful luxury liners, no crab boats or fishing vessels with seagulls in tow, not even the familiar Popeye Boat showing up to say goodbye.

A lull in the ordinarily rowdy wildlife activity that surrounded the pier had to be the reason for the unusual silence at the moment. There were no sea lions playing in the surf, the dolphins and porpoises were out to sea, and the pelicans, cormorants, and falcons had hunkered down for the day. Even the gulls had gone silent.

The wildlife and the vessels would return and maintain their routines as they had for many years and on into the future, but the colorful painters of years past who had long since retired would not. The mysterious Russian, the all-boy Roger, and my adversary Smokey were among the many characters who were forever gone from the Bridge, but they would not be forgotten.

I am very thankful for my years on the Bridge, and glad I took it all in. As far as being a Golden Gate Bridge painter, like most adventures in life, this job did not take the path I intended, but am proud to say that it never became "just a job." I love my beautiful Bridge as much today as I did the first time I met her, and my time spent there was nothing short of amazing, unique, and an absolute blast. The Bridge will live forever, and while Bridge painters will continue to come and go, they will never do it like we did. `

I was startled out of my reverie by the slam of the elevator door being opened, and I realized the laborer had returned. It was time to leave the pier. I took one last look around and saw that the fog had enveloped me. Other than the ground I stood on, I could see little more than a slight outline of the towers.

I turned and headed to the South Tower, hustled up the ladder rungs, stepped onto the platform, and gazed out at the expanse of fog. Finally, I turned in the direction of the now-invisible security door. I had just extended one leg into the oval-shaped opening and ducked my head to enter the tower when I was stopped mid-duck by a familiar thunderous roar coming from nearby. The mighty foghorn had sounded off for me one last time. My heart felt full, and I tilted my head back, blinking quickly and then squeezing my eyes shut as not to tear up. I climbed through the doorway, and as I turned to take one last look, the foghorn went off again. I couldn't contain the smile that crossed my face.

I softly called out, "Goodbye, South Tower Pier." With that, I pulled the door shut.

A VIEW THROUGH THE FOG

APPENDIX A:

GLOSSARY/BRIDGE TERMS

Abutment - A structure that supports the end of a bridge or a structure that anchors the cables of a suspension bridge.

Anchorage – The support structure for anchoring and holding the cable ends of a suspension bridge.

Arch – A structural device, forming the curved, pointed or flat upper edge of an opening or a support, as in a bridge.

Balustrade – A rail and row of posts (balusters) that support it, along the edge.

Box grinder – Deep hollow box beam which can have a rectangular or trapezoidal cross section.

Caisson – A watertight structure.

Chord – The top or bottom, horizontal part of a truss.

Cutwater – The end of a pier base that is pointed to cleave the water.

Eyebar – Unit from which the cables of a suspension bridge are constructed with a flattened ring at each end for linkages.

Flange – The top or bottom plate of a box girder or I-beam.

Girder – A large or deep horizontal beam, used as a main support for vertical loads.

Gusset plates – Triangular inserts, for strengthening and enlarging.

Hangers – Wires or bars from which the deck is hung on a suspension bridge, also known as suspenders.

I-beam – Beam or girder with an I shaped cross-section.

Mid-span – Spot where the main cables reach their lowest point.

Orthotropic – Tending to grow or form along a vertical axis.

Pier – A supporting structure at the junction of connecting spans of a bridge

Plate girder – Flat bridge deck with a shallow rectangular section.

Pylon – Vertical mast or tower above the bridge deck to which the cable stays are fixed.

Side spans – Outer or end spans of a suspension bridge from the tower to the anchorage, balancing the central suspended span.

Stay – To brace or support.

Stiffening truss – Truss supporting the entire deck of a suspension bridge.

Stringer – A long, heavy horizontal timber or steel beam used for any of several corrective or supportive purposes.

Strut – A bar or rod used to strengthen a framework by resisting longitudinal thrust.

Suspension bridge – A bridge with its deck supported by large cables draped from towers.

Tower – Vertical support structure of a suspension bridge from which the cables are hung.

Truss – A frame of tension and compression members, which together make up a long span beam.

Viaduct – Series of spans or arches used to carry a road or railroad over other roads or valleys.

Web – One of the side plates of a box grinder on the vertical plate of an I-beam.

APPENDIX B:
BRIDGE STATISTICS

THE BASICS

Total length of bridge, including approaches	8,981 ft.	(1.7 mi.) 2,737 m.
Length of suspension span including main span and side spans	6,450 ft.	(1.2 mi.) 1,966 m.
Length of suspension span excluding side spans4,	200 ft.	1,280 m.
Length of one side span	1,125 ft.	343 m.
Width of bridge	90 ft.	27 m.
Width of roadway between curbs *	62 ft.	19 m.
Width of sidewalk	10 ft.	3 m.
Clearance above mean high water	220 ft.	67 m.
Deepest foundation below mean low water	110 ft.	34 m.
Live load capacity per lineal foot	4,000 lbs.	1814.14 kg.

Maximum transverse deflection at center span	27.7 ft.	8.4 m.
Maximum downward deflection at center span	10.8 ft.	3.3 m.
Maximum upward deflection at center span	5.8 ft.	1.8 m.
Total weight of each anchorage 60,000 tons	109,000,000 kg.	
Total weight of bridge, anchorages and approaches (1937)	894,500 tons	811,500,000 kg.
Total weight of bridge, anchorages and approaches (1986)**	887,000 tons	804,700,000 kg.
Weight of bridge not including anchorages and approaches (1986)**	419,800 tons	380,800,000 kg.

MAIN TOWERS

Height of towers above water	746 ft.	227 m.
Height of towers above roadway	500 ft.	152 m.
Base dimension (each leg)	33 ft. x 54 ft.	10 m. x 16 m.
Weight of one tower	44,000 lbs.	40,200,000 kg.
Transverse deflection of towers	12.5 in.	0.32 m.

Longitudinal deflection of towers (shoreward)	22 in.	0.56 m.
Longitudinal deflection of towers (channelward)	18 in.	0.46 m.

MAIN CABLES

Diameter of cables including exterior wrapping	36 3/8 in.	0.92 m.
Length of one cable	7,650 ft.	2,332 m.
Total length of wire used	80,000 mi.	129,000 km.
Number of wires on each cable	27,572	
Number of strands in each cable	61	
Weight of main cables and suspender cables	24,500 tons	22,2000,000 kg.

STRUCTURAL STEEL QUANTITIES

Main towers	44,400 tons	40,280,000 kg.
Suspended structure	24,000 tons	21,772,000 kg.
Anchorages	4.400 tons	3,991,000 kg.
Approaches	10,200 tons	9,250,000 kg.

CONCRETE QUANTITIES (approx.)

	cubic yards	cubic meters
San Francisco pier and fender	130,000	99,400
Marin pier	23,500	18.000
Anchorages, pylons, and cable housing	182.000	139,160
Approaches	28,500	21,800

VEHICLE CROSSINGS

Annual vehicle crossings (northbound and southbound)	2018	39 million
Total vehicle crossings (northbound and southbound) since opening (as of July, 2019)		over 2.1 billion

TOLL REVENUE (approx.)

Annual toll revenue (fiscal year 2018/2019)	$152 million
Total toll revenue since opening (as of July 2019)	over $2 billion

* The roadway width was 60 feet when the bridge was constructed. The width was increased to 62 feet when new decking was completed in 1986.

** The total weight listed includes the reduction in weight due to the re-decking in 1986. The weight of the original reinforced concrete deck and its supporting stringers was 166.397 tons (150,592,000 kg). The weight of the new orthotropic steel plate deck, its two inches of epoxy asphalt surfacing, and its support pedestals is 154,093 tons (139,790,700 kg). This is a total weight reduction of the deck of 12,300 tons (11,158,400 kg), or 1.37 tons (1133 kg) per lineal foot of deck.

www.ingramcontent.com/pod-product-compliance
Lightning Source LLC
Chambersburg PA
CBHW041239240426
43668CB00022B/2441